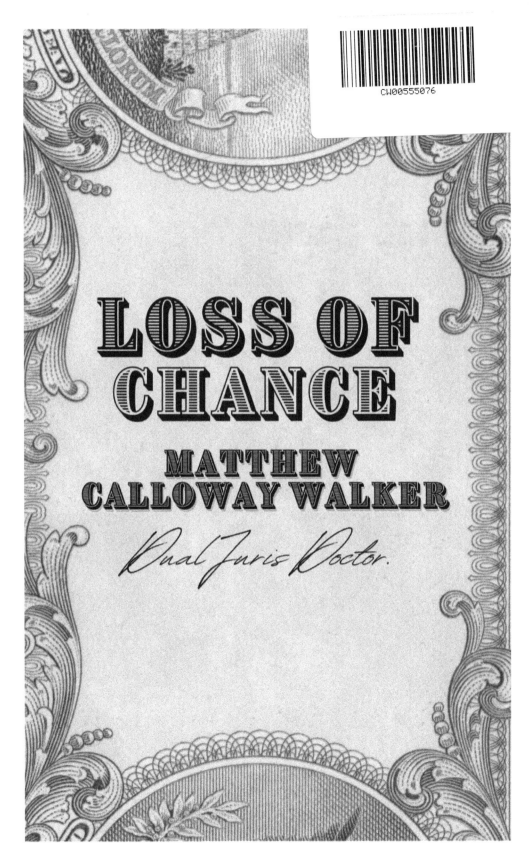

LOSS OF CHANCE

MATTHEW CALLOWAY WALKER

Dual Juris Doctor.

FOREWORD

LOSS OF CHANCE

It's late at night… I have just finished a long and demanding day, tending to my patients in my practice, and making the rounds at Humber River Hospital, and now my job, *as Mr. Walker has informed me*, is to tell you what exactly you've just gotten yourself into in purchasing this Book.

While for anyone else, I might refuse such a request, I have opted to make the rare exception in this situation, and for three very important reasons…

First, this book gets it right, and in more ways than one. From the medicine and his breakdown of the statistical methodology to his entertaining and methodical analogies, Matthew takes his readers on a fundamentally brilliant, compelling, and insightful journey into the world of medical malpractice. Secondly, Matthew manages to provide a perceptive and intuitive guide for not only individuals in his profession, but those like I, who are in the healthcare industry and want to learn more about the intricacies and nuances of the law. Additionally, the arguments Mathew advances are powerful, intelligently analytical, and significantly persuasive. For one faced with deciding whether to adopt the loss of chance doctrine, this may yet be the most valuable book you will ever read. This is the work of a masterful scholar and writer, who has a deep appreciation for law and medicine, and the core-competencies to back it up. By far, Matthew's account provides a detailed innovative approach that could have a revolutionary impact on the way the judicial system tackles medical malpractice and the loss of chance doctrine.

Finally, in writing this foreword, I am guaranteeing that for any future children Matthew decides to have, the first shall be named "Stephen."

My name is Dr. Stephen Glazer, and I am the Medical Director of the Surgical Bariatric Program at Humber River Regional Hospital and President of the Canadian Association of Physicians and Surgeons, and I have had the pleasure of knowing Matthew Walker for almost a decade, as mentor, friend, and supporter.

Stephen A. Glazer MD FRCPC FCCP

by
Matthew Calloway Walker
• Dual Juris Doctor •

WALKER

WALKER CREATIVE
Published by Walker Enterprises

First published in the United States; made available through:
Amazon United States; Amazon Canada; Amazon Japan; Amazon Australia; Amazon United Kingdom; Amazon Spain; Amazon Germany; Amazon France; Amazon Italy; Amazon Netherlands; Amazon Poland; Amazon Sweden.

Dedicated to *my mother*, Sam Walker,
My Hero
Protector
&
Best Friend
from 95' to infinity and beyond…

and to Lexi Callahan
My Champion
Tower of Strength
&
Counterpart in the Trenches

For Charlie, Steadman, Patterson, Lee and all others who thought I would only ever dribble a basketball.

A Note From The Author

From the bottom of my heart, thank you for purchasing this text.

A great deal of work and time went into making the publishing of this a reality. Hours spent pouring through research. Days filled with editing and formatting. Nights occupied by typing up chapters in the dark. And now… You have the chance to read something that has truly been a passion project of mine (*in truth, an obsession*) for many years. I hope you find this text insightful, easy to understand, and rewarding.

Thank you…

Books By Matthew Calloway Walker

Loss of Chance (2022).

Bending Realities: Introducing the Loss of Chance Doctrine into an Automated Multiverse of Madness (2023); and

Nano-Bots, Doctors in Disguise: Exploring Loss of Chance at the Nano-Level (2023).

PREFACE

This text is designed to be of both substantial scholarly and practical importance. While this text concerns itself with broad coverage of several countries across the Globe, *such as the United States, the United Kingdom, and Australia,* its initial focus was much more *confined. Simply,* it began as a passion project of mine in an effort to *bring balance* to the current system of tort in Canada. A passion which was ignited upon learning that out of 100 medical negligence cases, **55.2** will be *dismissed, discontinued,* or *abandoned;* **36.7** will be settled; **6.5** will be judgments found in favor of the physician; and only **1.6** will be in favor of the patient. These numbers were, and *remain* to this day, greatly troublesome to me, *and while many have argued a new judicial approach is needed,* arguably no true viable solution has been offered.

Imagine the Following Scenario:
You see a doctor, as you have been coughing up blood and fainting.
Unfortunately, the doctor fails to examine you thoroughly, tells you
it's anxiety, and in three months you learn you have cancer.
When you first saw the doctor, you had a 50% chance of living... but
three months have since passed, and you now have only a 10%
chance of living.
One month later... You die.

Many would agree, *and reasonably so,* that the physician in this scenario above caused you to lose a better chance to live, a chance to set your affairs in order, make things right with those you love, *etc.* But, as a plaintiff seeking redress, are you entitled to any recovery for this wrong suffered? **No, you get nothing** (*at least depending on which jurisdiction you find yourself in*).

The reality is, a number of courts across the Globe only award *full recovery* where the original chance lost was above 50%. Appreciably, this means that in the above scenario, you were only 1% away from full damages. This is not only *unjust* and *unequal* for the patient, but also for the physician...Why? It is grossly unfair to require a physician to pay full damages where a patient started out with 80% and dropped down to 70%. *Yet, that is the reality of today's system...*

Necessarily, this text is quite important, as it seeks to offer the solution to this problem. Specifically, I have crafted *multiple* solutions, which enable, *at varying levels*, equity for both *physician* and *patient*. This paper is authored by an individual with an accomplished academic background, having undertaken legal, health sciences, and psychology studies. *Notably*, what makes my perspective so valuable is my training in statistical analysis, as well as my ability to offer a unique *philosophical* and *theoretical* analysis. While other texts on this subject have offered a critique or review of case law or another's work, this text seeks to offer a single comprehensive review and a mathematically sound answer.

For those of whom read this text, it is meant to be a tool — after you set it down in completion, you should be able to understand what loss of chance is, where it came from, how it developed, and how it can be introduced in your jurisdiction. But, in order to get you to that point of knowledge, *context is key*. Not surprisingly, the loss of chance doctrine is very complex and quite encumbered by flawed math, and thus, to truly understand the value of what I present to you in the end, you need to know where we came from... you need to see the problems with our current system... and how we got here. Otherwise, *and sadly so*, you miss the whole picture. Moreover, it is extremely easy to reject an approach when you do not understand its *value* or the context within which it resides.

But still, you may ponder: *why is this text in particular quite so very valuable?* **The Answer** (*if you require yet another*): this text attempts to enable judges, academics, professionals, *and the like*, to turn to one single document to understand everything about loss of chance.

As a lawyer, judge, student, or interested party, think of how valuable it would be to have one secondary source that provides you with everything you need.

Ultimately, this text proffers a globe perspective, *not simply a review.* Many courts often look to foreign laws for guidance, and thus, think of the value in being able to see how a number of jurisdictions across the globe have approached and utilized this doctrine.

To efficiently convince someone that change needs to happen, *or simply that an approach needs to be adopted,* an authority has to exist, which covers the history, development, and application of this doctrine.

This sets out to be that Authority…

ACKNOWLEDGEMENT

First, I would like to thank Dr. Stephen Glazer for being such an incredible supporter of mine throughout the years. If ever I needed Dr. Glazer, he was there, guiding me, protecting me, and ensuring that I had the tools to be happy and successful in life. The quality of his character is of the highest, and his friendship is worth that of 1 million relatives. For these reasons, and so many more, I feel privileged and truly proud to call him my friend. Additionally, there are a handful of individuals who ought to be recognized. Should you see a name listed below, know that this is an individual who made an impact in my life for the better, from believing in me and showing me kindness and friendship to inspiring me and showing me the way...

Dr. Ira Bernstein
Mr. Vince Carter
Dean Jennifer Carter-Johnson
Mr. Walter Davidson, R.I.P.
Dean Carrie Feeheley
Dr. Bonnie Glencross
Mr. Randy Katzman
Dr. Pierre Kory
Scott Marsland, FNP
Professor Donald Morgenson, R.I.P.
Dr. Elizabeth Olds
Professor Philip Pucillo
Dr. Harvey Risch
Mr. Caleb Sandoval, R.I.P.
Dr. Dana Sawchuk
Professor Gehan Senthinathan
Miss Sonya
Dean Abijah Taylor
Dr. Joseph Varon
Mr. Tony Young

Saying thank you is simply not enough...

Table of Contents

Statistical Wizardry - Matthew's Loss of Chance
delivers in so many ways, well-crafted,
mathematically sound, uncomplicated, and a true
page turner in every sense of the word.
- Randy Katzman, B. Comm, CPA CA, CVLA
Chief Financial Officer (Roy Foss)

FOR WHOM THE BELL TOLLS

With every diagnosis given and every treatment prescribed, patients find themselves confined to operate on a metaphorical chess-board encumbered by statistics. There is virtually no liberation. *"How long do I have?" "Is it fatal?" "What are my options?" "What is my chance of survival?"* These are the quintessential queries which preoccupy and burden the mind. For any given patient, diagnosis and prognosis offer insight and to some extent clarity. Such information, offers the topographical map of which the patient must now traverse. However, it is statistical evaluation which can afford, *in the words of the late Dr. Stephen J. Gould*, "that most precious of all possible gifts in the circumstances—substantial time."[1]

Unfortunately, this reality is *oft* never realized when patients are subjected to negligent misdiagnosis. Under the shroud of wrongful error, the patient loses a statistical advantage pertaining to their

---

[1] *See* Stephen Jay Gould, *The Median Isn't the Message*, 15 Am. Assoc. J. Ethics 77, 77-81 (2013).

survival or recovery. Consideration of this loss of chance — *as compensable at law* — has sparked prodigious debate amongst legal scholars and judicial decision makers spanning the globe. As medical malpractice actions in some countries have seen a decline in patient claim success over the past 40 years, many have argued a new judicial approach is needed.[2] One approach offered is to utilize *the loss of chance doctrine*, which provides proportionate compensation to an aggrieved party who, *through negligent misdiagnosis*, lost a chance ($\leq 50\%$) for a better outcome.[3] While this approach is quite appealing, many jurisdictions have rejected its application, only awarding damages where the chance lost surpasses a 50% threshold.[4] *Ergo*, recovery for a patient with a 51% chance of survival at the time of negligent misdiagnosis is permissible, *whereas*, recovery would be precluded for a patient with an initial 49% chance.[5] This approach is opposite to the United States, where 26 states have not only recognized this doctrine's value but accepted it as compensable.[6]

---

[2] *See, e.g.,* Habiba Nosheen & Andrew Culbert, *As fewer patients sue their doctor, the rate of winning malpractice suits is dropping too*, CBC (Apr. 18, 2019), www.cbc.ca/news/health/medical-malpractice-doctors-lawsuits-canada-1.4913960; Douglas Danner, *1 Med. Malprac. Chklsts. & Disc. § 1:11*, Westlaw (database updated Sept. 2021) ("Statistics show that 95% of all medical malpractice cases are dropped, settled or otherwise disposed of before trial. Of the 5% which go to trial, the defendants win about half of these cases."); Adam C. Schaffer, et al., *Rates and Characteristics of Paid Malpractice Claims Among US Physicians by Specialty*, 1992-2014, JAMA Intern Med. 717 (2017).

[3] Paul Fangrow, *Will Loss of Chance Doctrine Lose its Chance in North Carolina?*, Wake Forest Law Review: Current Issues Blog (Sept. 10, 2019), http://www.wakeforestlawreview.com/2019/09/will-loss-of-chance-doctrine-lose-its-chance-in-north-carolina/; Lauren Guest et al., *The "Loss of Chance" Rule As A Special Category of Damages in Medical Malpractice: A State-by-State Analysis*, 21-APR J. Legal Econ. 53 (2015); *Dickhoff ex rel. Dickhoff v. Green*, 836 N.W.2d 321, 344 (Minn. 2013); and *Matsuyama v. Birnbaum*, 452 Mass. 1, 10 (2008), *abrogated by Doull v. Foster*, 487 Mass. 1 (2021).

[4] Joan F. Renehan, *A New Frontier: The Loss of Chance Doctrine in Medical Malpractice Cases*, 53-JUN Boston B.J. 14, 15 (2009); Guest, *supra* note 3; 836 N.W.2d at 344; 452 Mass. at 10; *Cottrelle v. Gerrard*, 2003 CanLII 50091 (ON CA); *Laferrière v. Lawson*, 1991 CanLII 87 (SCC); *Gregg v. Scott*, [2005] UKHL 2; and Harold Luntz, *Loss of Chance in Medical Negligence*, Uni. Mel. Law Sch. Leg. Studies Res. Pap. Ser. (2011).

[5] *Supra* note 3.

[6] 836 N.W.2d 321; *Alberts v. Schultz*, 126 N.M. 807 (1999); *Delaney v. Cade*, 255 Kan. 199, 218 (1994); *Hamil v. Bashline*, 481 Pa. 256 (1978); *Est. of Frey v. Mastroianni*, 146 Haw. 540 (2020); *Wollen v. DePaul Health Ctr.*, 828 S.W.2d 681 (Mo. 1992); *DeBurkarte v. Louvar*, 393 N.W.2d 131 (Iowa 1986); *Ferrell v. Rosenbaum*, 691 A.2d 641 (D.C. 1997);

This text attempts to gather the relevant literature and proposals concerning *the loss of chance doctrine*, organizing them in a way that is coherent and understandable. In doing so, the hopeful objective is to proffer this writing as somewhat of a "Silmarillion", *i.e., an authority, covering the history and development of this doctrine*, giving heed to its consideration *via* the courts. Necessarily, this text begins by detailing the history and evolution of negligence law, identifying the difficulties in proving causation, and then exploring how the loss of chance doctrine has been considered globally. I then detail the opposing views of two scholars, after which I offer my personal critique, and four of my own approaches that I crafted: *the Traditional Doctrine+, Pro Rata Extremus, the Walker Approach, and the Tantalus Alternative Test.*

We must, however, remember at all times the application of any proposal is dependent on the views of each jurisdiction.

It should be noted—*I simply aim to offer an analytical critique through an empirical and philosophical approach, designed to offer an objective opinion in an area of debate which is so subjectively hampered.*[7]

Cahoon v. Cummings, 734 N.E.2d 535 (Ind. 2000); *McMackin v. Johnson Cnty. Healthcare Ctr.*, 2003 WY 91 (Wyo. 2003), *on reh'g* 2004 WY 44 (Wyo. 2004); *Perez v. Las Vegas Med. Ctr.*, 107 Nev. 1 (1991); *Smith v. Providence Health & Servs.-Oregon*, 361 Or. 456 (2017); *McKellips v. Saint Francis Hosp., Inc.*, 1987 OK 69 (1987); *Thompson v. Sun City Cmty. Hosp., Inc.*, 141 Ariz. 597 (1984); *Hastings v. Baton Rouge Gen. Hosp.*, 498 So. 2d 713 (La. 1986); Fangrow, *supra* note 3; Guest, *supra* note 3; and Charles Jones et al., *"The Loss of Chance" Doctrine in Medical Malpractice Cases*, Troutman Pepper (Mar. 13, 2013), www.troutman.com/insights/the-loss-of-chance-doctrine-in-medical-malpractice-cases.html.

[7] *See* Robert Solomon et al., *Cases and Materials on the Law of Torts* 1151 (Carswell 9th ed. 2015).

Chapter 2

BACK TO THE FUTURE

Contrary to what many have presupposed, cause of action in claims of negligence are ambiguous, with scope principally influenced by the judiciary's interpretation of the duty of care.[8] "The threshold issue" for any plaintiff making a negligence claim is whether the plaintiff was owed a duty of care by the wrongdoer.[9] Historically, there has been a shift, with many jurisdictions having moved to a more conservative approach from one favoring plaintiffs.[10]

Exploring Negligence— The historical roots of negligence law can be traced back to when courts began to recognize that there were circumstances in which damages ought to be awarded where a wrongdoer has indirectly done harm to a plaintiff.[11] Initially, the early writ system only accommodated plaintiffs who, *in bringing their claim of trespass vi et armis*, could prove a direct injury.[12] In such cases, defendants would generally be precluded from liability if they

---

[8] *Id.* at 293.
[9] *Id.*; Dan B. Dobbs et al., *The Law of Torts § 125* (2d ed.), Westlaw (database updated July 2022).
[10] Solomon, *supra* note 8; Guest, *supra* note 3; Fangrow, *supra* note 3; Dobbs, *supra* note 9, at § 196; and [2005] UKHL 2.
[11] Solomon, *supra* note 8.
[12] *Id.*; Dobbs, *supra* note 9, at § 17.

could establish that any damage caused was not the *resultant* of their own commission.[13] However, trespass *vi et armis* was too narrow, failing to capture findings of liability where there was no directness or forcefulness, and yet loss had occurred.[14] Appreciably, this changed with the development and eventual furtherance of the writ of *trespass on the case*, as plaintiffs could now seek remedy under an assortment of actions, having only to establish actual loss and negligent or intentional behavior.[15] Thus, *under negligence*, tortfeasors were aptly held accountable for their carelessness.[16] However, *initially*, liability was narrowly imposed so as to capture only those individuals, for whom it could be said breached requisite standards necessarily dictated by their relative professions.[17]

As a means of controlling the *flexibility* of negligence law, courts held that relief would only be granted if a finding of fault could be attributed to the tortfeasor's failing to meet an identifiable standard of care.[18] However, this adapted version of the standard of customary practice rarely was extended beyond those categories which were recognized and established by the judiciary.[19] Thus, *essentially* — if precedence was non-existent — a plaintiff would be unable to bring a successful claim in negligence.[20]

---

[13] Solomon, *supra* note 8.

[14] *Id.*

[15] *Id.* at 294; Dobbs, *supra* note 12.

[16] *Id.*

[17] Solomon, *supra* note 8, at 294.

[18] *Id.*; Dobbs, *supra* note 9, at § 121.

[19] Solomon, *supra* note 17; and *see also* Dobbs, *supra* note 9, at § 121.

[20] Solomon, *supra* note 17.

The Big Bang—It wasn't until 1932 that a broader duty of care in negligence was recognized and established by the U.K. case *Donoghue v. Stevenson*.[21] In *Donoghue*, Lord Atkin delivered what many consider to be *one of the most influential judgements in negligence law*, as he established the principles upon which modern negligence law has come to rely:

I.	The existence of a duty of care can be extended to <u>any</u> <u>situation</u>;
II.	tortfeasors can be held liable for omissions for which injury was reasonably foreseeable; ***and***
III.	a breach of the standard of care must be shown, as alone, the duty of care is insufficient.[22]

This decision in *Donoghue*, resulted in negligence law being available to plaintiffs who, *priorly*, were precluded and dissuaded from bringing an action in negligence.[23] Notably, *as a means for persuasive support*, Lord Atkin cited *MacPherson v. Buick Motor Co.*, 217 N.Y. 382 (1916), the decision which "liberated the common law of negligence in the United States from its traditional constraints."[24]

---

[21] *Id.*; and Allan C. Hutchinson, *Some "What If" Thoughts: Notes on Donoghue v Stevenson*, 51 Osgoode Hall L. J. 706 (2014) ("*Donoghue* is an extension of a principle that Justice Benjamin Cardozo articulated in 1916 in the American case of *MacPherson v Buick Motor Co.*").

[22] Solomon, *supra* note 17, at 295 and 304-8; and *Donoghue v. Stevenson*, [1932] AC 562, SC (HL) 31.

[23] Solomon, *supra* note 17, at 312.

[24] Franz Werro & Claudia Hasbun, *Is Macpherson A Legacy of Civilian Views?*, 9 J. Tort L. 67, 89 and 74 (2016) ("*MacPherson* explicitly influenced one of the most cited English decisions in tort law, *Donoghue v. Stevenson*").

THE BASIC ELEMENTS

In seeking to bring a viable claim in medical negligence, it is for the plaintiff to establish the following elements are present:

I. *the defendant owed a duty of care,*

II. *the standard of care was breached by the defendant,*

III. *the plaintiff sustained a loss, and*

IV. *the loss or damage was caused by the defendant's breach.*[25]

Notably, *remoteness* "seldom arises in medical cases," but allows the court to determine whether the loss was reasonably foreseeable.[26]

---

[25] 836 N.W.2d 321; 126 N.M. 807; 255 Kan. 199; 481 Pa. 256; 146 Haw. 540; 828 S.W.2d 681; 393 N.W.2d 131; 691 A.2d 641; 734 N.E.2d 535; 2003 WY 91; 107 Nev. 1 (1991); 361 Or. 456; 1987 OK 69; 141 Ariz. 597; 498 So. 2d 713; Solomon, *supra* note 17, at 297; Joanna Erdman et al., *Canadian Health Law and Policy* 307 (LexisNexis Canada, 5th ed. 2017); and *Saadati v. Moorhead*, 2017 SCC 28.

[26] Erdman, *supra* note 25, at 315; and Solomon, *supra* note 25, at 297.

EXCULPATORY BUT FOR

In the realm of medical negligence, it is relatively not burdensome for a *patient-plaintiff* to satisfy that a duty of care is owed—*it being well-established that medical professionals owe such duties to their patients.*[27] Conversely, what truly can become arduous, *and oft does*, for most *patient-plaintiffs*, is tackling the steep acclivity that presents with the issue of proving causation.[28]

NAVIGATING CAUSAL UNCERTAINTY IN MEDICAL NEGLIGENCE

In the context of medical negligence, the general test applied in proving causation requires the plaintiff to evidence that their injury(*ies*) would not have resulted "but for" the physician's negligence.[29] Notably, the purpose of this test is twofold, existing as

---

[27] Erdman, *supra* note 25; Dobbs, *supra* note 9, at § 285; and Solomon, *supra* note 25, at 438.

[28] 452 Mass. at 12; Renehan, *supra* note 4; Joseph King, *Causation, Valuation, and Chance in Personal Injury Torts Involving Preexisting Conditions and Future Consequences*, 90 Yale L.J. 1353, 1356 (1981); and *Bigwood v. Bos.*, 209 Mass. 345, 348 (1911); Erdman et al., *supra* note 26; Ernest J. Weinrib, *Causal Uncertainty*, 36 Oxford J. Leg. Stud. 135 (2016); Vaughan Black, *The Rise and Fall of the Plaintiff-friendly Causation*, 53 Alta. L. Rev. 1014 (2016); Solomon, *supra* note 17, at 602-18; 836 N.W.2d at 344; Dobbs, *supra* note 9, at § 186 ("In a number of cases, however, the but-for test of factual cause puts the plaintiff out of court, even though the defendant is clearly negligent."); and Guest, *supra* note 3.

[29] King, *supra* note 28, at 1355; Dobbs, *supra* note 9, at § 186; 2003 CanLII 50091; *Civil Liability Act 2002 No. 22* (NSW) § 5D; *Civil Liability Act 2002* (TAS) § 13; *Civil Liability Act 2003* (Qld) § 11; *Wrongs Act 1958* (VIC) § 51; *Civil Liability Act 1936* (SA) § 34; *Civil*

both an exculpatory tool if left unsatisfied by the plaintiff — and if satisfied — as a tool affirming culpability.[30] Thus, in establishing this "but for" test, liability can be "justifiably" imposed, as the test allows for the requisite link between *the wrong suffered* and *the wrongdoer* to be factually recognized.[31] A pivotal issue arising in many medical cases, is the factual uncertainty inherent in the circumstances of any given case, which can make finding a causal link insuperable.[32]

Consequently, in addressing the many *plaintiff-centered* concerns regarding the unfair burden implicit in handling such uncertainties, the courts have had to contend with how liability ought to be established in a manner that is fair.[33] For instance, the Supreme Court of Canada has addressed these concerns by considering whether changes to the "but for" test were warranted to enable such plaintiffs to recover.[34] Specifically, in *Snell v. Farrell*, 2 SCR 311 (1990), The Supreme Court of Canada was tasked with deciding whether a departure from the "but for" test was merited in situations where plaintiff suffered an injury, but could not establish causation.[35] Justice Sopinka, *delivering judgement on behalf of the Court*, found that in cases of medical negligence, medical certainty is not necessary in establishing a finding of causation.[36] Generally, all that is required is that it be shown *on a balance of probabilities (or preponderance of*

Law (Wrongs) Act 2002 (ACT) § 45; and *Civil Liability Act 2002* (WA) § 5C; Luntz, *supra* note 4, at 12; and Xiaowei Yu, *Causal Uncertainty in Chinese Medical Malpractice Law - When Theories Meet Facts*, 9 Tsinghua China L. Rev. 23, 33 (2016).

[30] Erdman, *supra* note 26; Solomon, *supra* note 17, at 596; Nayha Acharya, *No More Chances for Lost Chances: A Weinribian Response to Weinrib*, 12 McGill J. L. & Health 205 (2019); and Dobbs, supra note 9, at § 186.

[31] *Id.*

[32] Renehan, *supra* note 4; Acharya, *supra* note 30, at 207-08; 452 Mass. at 12; King, *supra* note 28; Yu, *supra* note 29, at 31; and 209 Mass. at 348.

[33] Renehan, *supra* note 4; 209 Mass. at 348; Acharya, *supra* note 32; 452 Mass. at 12; Yu, *supra* note 29, at 30-33; Luntz, *supra* note 4, at 25; and King, *supra* note 28.

[34] Solomon, *supra* note 17 at 602-18; *Snell v. Farrell*, 2 SCR 311 (1990); *Resurfice Corp. v. Hanke*, 1 SCR 333 (2007); *Clements v. Clements*, 2012 SCC 32; and Acharya, *supra* note 30, at 208-09.

[35] Solomon, *supra* note 17 at 604; and 2 SCR 311.

[36] Solomon, *supra* note 35; 2 SCR 311; and Dobbs, *supra* note 9, at § 191 (showing that the same principle applies in the United States).

the evidence) (*i.e.,* 51% *or more*) that the defendant was the cause.[37] However, in medical malpractice cases, it is a frequent occurrence that the defendant, *as the patient-plaintiff's physician*, is in a better position to ascertain "cause," with respect to the injuries sustained.[38] Appreciably, such a state of affairs has led to the question: *should the burden of proof shift to the defendant in such cases*.[39] Unfalteringly, the law in general is clear, the ultimate burden lies with the plaintiff.[40] However, causation may be inferred though no affirming *nor* scientific proof is provided.[41] Ultimately, it is the law upon which judgements are to be based.[42]

THE MATERIAL CONTRIBUTION TEST — sticking with Canada for the moment, *as an alternative to the "but for" test*, in 1996 the Supreme Court of Canada introduced the material contribution test in *Athey v. Leonati*, 3 SCR 458 (1996), a test later applied in *Walker*

---

[37] Solomon, *supra* note 35; 2 SCR 311; and *1653. Preponderance of Evidence*, West's ALR Digest Negligence k1653 (Nov. 2021 Update). Notably, there is no difference between the terms *balance of probabilities* and *preponderance of the evidence*. Both terms refer to equivalent standards, being *more likely than not* (51% or more). The United States utilizes the *preponderance* terminology, whereas Canada and the United Kingdom rely on the *balance of probabilities* phraseology. Comparably, Chinese law has adopted a much greater standard of proof, with some claiming it to be at least 70%. However, it being left to each judge's discretion, such high probability has not been utilized in practice, as members of the Chinese judiciary often employ or equate the Chinese standard of proof with the preponderance standard. *See* Yu, *supra* note 29, at 36 and n. 60.

[38] Solomon, *supra* note 35; and Yu, *supra* note 29, at 28-29.

[39] Solomon, *supra* note 35; Yu, *supra* note 29, at 34; and Luntz, *supra* note 33.

[40] Solomon, *supra* note 35; Dobbs, *supra* note 9, at § 183; *Preponderance of Evidence, supra* note 37; Yu, *supra* note 39; *Civil Liability Act 2002 No. 22* (NSW) § 5E; *Civil Liability Act 2002* (TAS) § 14; *Civil Liability Act 2003* (Qld) § 12; *Wrongs Act 1958* (VIC) § 52; *Civil Liability Act 1936* (SA) § 35; *Civil Law (Wrongs) Act 2002* (ACT) § 46; *Civil Liability Act 2002* (WA) § 5D; and Luntz, *supra* note 33, at 27 ("The High Court of Australia refused to modify the requirement that the plaintiff in such an action must prove on the balance of probabilities that the defendant's negligence caused or contributed to the occurrence of the physical harm of which the plaintiff complains.").

[41] 2 SCR 311 (holding that causation may be inferred though no affirming nor scientific proof is provided); and Dobbs, *supra* note 9, at § 191.

[42] Solomon, *supra* note 35; and *TC by his tutor Sabatino v New South Wales & Ors*, [2001] NSWCA 380, para. 66 ("Questions of causation are not answered in a legal vacuum. Rather, they are answered in the legal framework in which they arise. For present purposes, that framework is the law of negligence.").

Estate v. York Finch General Hospital, 2001 SCC 23.[43] Unfortunately, in both cases the Supreme Court of Canada failed to clearly define what the material contribution to injury test meant or when it would be applied.[44] In fact, clarification on this test was not actually provided until 2007, when the Supreme Court of Canada held in *Resurfice Corp. v. Hanke*, 1 SCR 333 (2007) that this test would apply only if the plaintiff established: the impossibility of using the "but for" test to prove causation due to factors outside of their control; and that the defendant breached the standard of care, with the loss sustained being *within the scope of risk* resulting from that breach.[45] Unfortunately, *Hanke,* too, failed to define the meaning of the *material contribution test*.[46] Thus, confusion arose as to whether the test as outlined, referred to risk of injury or contribution to injury.[47]

Five years later, this test was revisited by the Supreme Court of Canada, in *Clements v. Clements*, 2012 SCC 32, a case which many Canadian judicial scholars recognize as the ultimate authority on material contribution, as it was here that the Supreme Court had the opportunity to clarify the law regarding causation and the "but for" test.[48] Not surprisingly, this Court reaffirmed *Snell*, and held that as a default rule, the "but for" test still stands as all-mighty.[49] Consequently, material contribution "remains" so as only to be applied to circumstances where multiple negligent defendants are

---

[43] Solomon, *supra* note 17 at 611; *Athey v. Leonati*, 3 SCR 458 (1996); and *Walker Estate v. York Finch General Hospital*, 2001 SCC 23.

[44] Solomon, *supra* note 43; 3 SCR 458; 2001 SCC 23; Black, *supra* note 28, at 1018 ("Presumably, the material contribution test was more plaintiff-favouring than the "but for" test, but beyond that *Athey* said nothing about what it meant and moreover nothing helpful about when this new (or at least new to Canada) alternative test might be available."); and for UK, *see Thorley v. Sandwell & West Birmingham Hospitals NHS Trust*, [2021] EWHC 2604 (QB), at para. 151 ("Accordingly the claim of material contribution must fail on the basis that this modified test of causation does not apply when there is a single tortfeasor and an indivisible injury.").

[45] Solomon, *supra* note 17, at 611-12; and 1 SCR 333, at para. 25.

[46] *Id.*

[47] *Id.*

[48] 2012 SCC 32; Black, *supra* note 28, at 1018-19; and Samantha Galway & Gordon McKee, *Causation in Canada Revisited: Material Contribution to Risk and the Impact of Clements (Litigation Guardian of) v. Clements*, 83 Def. Couns. J. 487 (2016).

[49] 2012 SCC 32, at para. 29; Black, *supra* note 28, at 1021; and Galway, *supra* note 48.

involved, with "all the putative causes to be tortious."[50] Understandably, application to such limited a context is justified, as the defense against causation offers that the cause of injury can be attributed to another *tortfeasor*, precluding plaintiff from attributing injury to any one of the defendants.[51] However, in the modern Canadian negligence context, this test is to a large extent extinct, if not practically unusable.[52] Although, *theoretically* it can still be used, from an extremely pragmatic standpoint, it has never been applied by the Supreme Court of Canada after its discussion in *Clements*.[53] Moreover, from in-depth review of the Canadian tort case law, desuetude is further apparent, as any time the *material contribution test* has been applied in any Canadian court, it has been overturned, or proven an *error* upon appeal thereafter.[54]

THE COURTS RESISTANCE TO CHANGE

Notably, while the above discussion relates to how Canada alone has grappled with the "but for" test, upon a *multi-jurisdictional* survey of the case law, the judiciaries' resistance to modifying the "but for" test (*or adopting new procedures that might remove barriers imposed by causal uncertainties*) becomes, *similarly*, quite transpicuous.

Ultimately, four fundamental principles have emerged from the case law across jurisdictions. First, the "but for" test remains the default test for causation.[55] Secondly, scientific certainty is not

---

[50] 2012 SCC 32 at para. 13 (limiting material contribution to "where it is impossible to determine which of a number of negligent acts by multiple actors in fact caused the injury, but it is established that one or more of them did in fact cause it."); Black, *supra* note 28, at 1022 and 1027; and Galway, *supra* note 48.

[51] 2012 SCC 32 at para. 13 and 18 (referring to "the classic 'point the finger at someone else' defence": "the goals of tort law and the underlying theory of corrective justice require that the defendant not be permitted to escape liability by pointing the finger at another wrongdoer."); and Galway, *supra* note 48, at 490-91.

[52] Galway, *supra* note 48, at 493-95; and Black, *supra* note 28, at 1027.

[53] *Id.*

[54] Galway, *supra* note 52; Black, *supra* note 52; *Dawes v. Gill*, 2019 ONSC 5649; and *Donleavy v. Ultramar Ltd.*, 2019 ONCA 687.

[55] Civil Liability Act 2002 No 22 (NSW) § 5D; Civil Liability Act 2002 (TAS) § 13; Civil Liability Act 2003 (Qld) § 11 Wrongs Act 1958 (VIC) § 51; Civil Liability Act 1936 (SA) § 34; Civil Law (Wrongs) Act 2002 (ACT) § 45; Civil Liability Act 2002 (WA) § 5C;

required to prove causation.[56] Thirdly, *in the context of increased risk*, the burden does not shift to the defendant to disprove a presumption of causation. Rather, the burden remains with the plaintiff who must, *as a matter of fact*, establish the physician's negligence resulted in a material increase in risk.[57] Necessarily, if it can be shown that the defendant created a risk, one which was more than likely the cause of the injury sustained, such will suffice.[58] Lastly, courts must take a "robust and pragmatic approach" to causation.[59]

Causation, Practical Law UK Glossary, Westlaw UK (last visited Aug. 25, 2022); Mark Brookes et al., *The 'but for' test of causation in Australian law*, Carter Newell (Dec. 2020), https://www.carternewell.com/page/Publications/2020/the-but-for-test-of-causation-in-australian-law/ ("The various Civil Liability Acts confirm that factual causation requires the answering of the 'but for' causal question."); Galway, *supra* note 48, at 488; Black, *supra* note 52 ("[I]t is a "but for" world out there."); 2012 SCC 32, at para. 46 ("As a general rule, a plaintiff cannot succeed unless she shows as a matter of fact that she would not have suffered the loss "but for" the negligent act or acts of the defendant."); Acharya, *supra* note 30, at 207; and Peter M. Willcock & James M. Lepp, *Causation in Medical Negligence Cases*, at 1, The Canadian Bar Association (2008), http://www.cba.org/cba/cle/pdf/Causation in Medical Negligence Cases_paper.pdf.

[56] Dobbs, *supra* note 9, at § 191; 2 SCR 311; Black, *supra* note 28, at 1028; Erdman, *supra* note 26, at 316; Dympna Devenney, *In the absence of scientific certainty pointing towards a cause, the court must rely on the varying and contrasting professional opinions as to what occurred*, 27 M.L.J.I. 2021, at 96 (2021); *Briggs v. IAG Ltd. t/a NRMA Insur.*, [2022] NSWSC 372, at para. 70; *Seltsam Pty. Ltd. v. McGuiness*, [2000] NSWCA 29, at para. 143 ("An inference of causation for purposes of the tort of negligence may well be drawn when a scientist, including an epidemiologist, would not draw such an inference."); and *Metro North Hosp. and Health Service v. Pierce*, [2018] NSWCA 11, at para. 138 ("Whether the Hospital's negligence in not responding to the induced seizures in a timely manner materially contributed to Ms[.] Pierce's worsened condition is not to be determined on the basis of scientific certainty, but on the balance of probabilities.").

[57] 2 SCR 311; Solomon, *supra* note 17, at 604-11; Black, *supra* note 28, at 1021; Dobbs, *supra* note 9, at § 183; Preponderance of Evidence, *supra* note 37; Civil Liability Act 2002 No. 22 (NSW) § 5E; Civil Liability Act 2002 (TAS) § 14; Civil Liability Act 2003 (Qld) § 12; Wrongs Act 1958 (VIC) § 52; Civil Liability Act 1936 (SA) § 35; Civil Law (Wrongs) Act 2002 (ACT) § 46; and Civil Liability Act 2002 (WA) § 5D.

[58] 2 SCR 311; Solomon, *supra* note 17, at 611; and Restatement (Third) of Torts: Phys. & Emot. Harm § 3 (2010), Westlaw (database updated May 2022).

[59] 2 SCR 311; 2012 SCC 32; Erdman, *supra* note 56; Acharya, *supra* note 30, at 208; Black, *supra* note 28, at 1016; and [2001] NSWCA at para. 63.

AMAZON'S #1 NEW RELEASE IN TORTS LAW

"While I can go-on and on about how great this book is, it suffices to say that this book just reads magnificently and offers something so unique and enjoyable outside of what is currently available on the market.

Randy Katzman, B. Comm, CPA CA, CVLA
Chief Financial Officer Roy Foss

Chapter 5

THE LOSS OF CHANCE DOCTRINE

The loss of chance doctrine was the main-attraction in the seminal U.K. contracts case *Chaplin v. Hicks,* [1911] 2 K.B. 786.[60] Specifically, the plaintiff was selected amongst fifty others to be interviewed by the defendant for a chance to receive an acting contract. Unfortunately, the plaintiff lost this chance, as she was out of town when notice was sent. Consequently, the plaintiff argued "reasonable steps" were not taken to allow her to present "herself for selection."[61] Accordingly, the plaintiff brought a claim against the defendant for *loss of chance of selection*, and was awarded damages, as it was held that the plaintiff was deprived "of something which had a monetary value."[62] Notably, presiding Lord Justice Williams held, the mere fact that *"damages cannot be assessed with certainty does not relieve the wrong-doer of the necessity of paying damages for his breach of contract."*[63]

Further, *Chaplin* proffered that in the face of multifarious contingencies, it should not be that of the default to preclude a plaintiff from recovery of damages. Accordingly, this court asserted that any

---

[60] Stephanie Ben-Ishai & David R. Percy, *Contracts: Cases and Commentaries*, 822-24 (10th ed. Carswell 2018); and *Chaplin v. Hicks,* [1911] 2 K.B. 786.
[61] *Id.*
[62] *Id.*
[63] *Id.*

decision maker must do the "best" that they can, though the presence of such contingencies may render valuation of the loss difficult to achieve with certainty.[64] *In other words*, *Chaplin* expresses <u>both</u> the sentiment and understanding that the final verdict reached might be no more than a variation of guesswork.[65] Appreciably, I hereby submit that the importation of this doctrine, *as applied above in contract law*, has faced much criticism, across the Globe, in the context of medical negligence.[66]

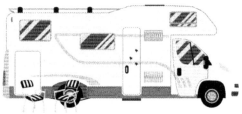

FAILING TO KNOCK: THE CASE OF MR. WHITE

Apparent from the four previously stated principles, a plaintiff — *in the context of medical negligence* — must establish the injury they suffered would not have occurred "but for" the physician's negligence.[67] However, often all the plaintiff is able to establish is that their physician's negligence denied them a chance for recovery or survival.[68] In these circumstances, some courts have restricted awarding damages to only those plaintiffs who had an initial chance which surpassed 50%.[69] This restriction has sparked great debate, with many arguing proportionate recovery is justifiably owed where the

---

[64] *Id.*

[65] *Id.*

[66] Renehan, *supra* note 4, at 14; 452 Mass. at 14; Black, *supra* note 28, at 1017 (stating that the loss of chance doctrine is greatly controversial in Canada and has been "comprehensively rejected in cases of medical negligence"); Luntz, *supra* note 4, at 6; Ben-Ishai *supra* note 60, at 824; *Gooding v. Univ. Hosp. Bldg., Inc.*, 445 So. 2d 1015, at 1019 (Fla. 1984); Acharya, *supra* note 30; and [2005] UKHL 2, at para. 226 ("The complexities of attempting to introduce liability for the loss of a chance of a more favourable outcome in personal injury claims have driven me, not without regret, to conclude that it should not be done.").

[67] *See* 2003 CanLII 50091; Luntz, *supra* note 4; King, *supra* note 28, at 1355; [2005] UKHL 2, at para. 15; and Dobbs, *supra* note 9, at § 186.

[68] 452 Mass. at 12; Renehan, *supra* note 4; 836 N.W.2d at 344; Luntz, *supra* note 4; and *see generally* Guest, *supra* note 3.

[69] 2003 CanLII 50091; Luntz, *supra* note 4; and Guest, *supra* note 3.

initial chance lost was below 50%.[70]

The following scenario is to be considered:

Mr. White presents to his family physician, *Dr. Goodman,* experiencing adverse symptoms often correlative with laryngeal cancer. Unfortunately, Dr. Goodman has misplaced Mr. White's medical history, *and thus,* is completely unaware of either Mr. White's exposure to chemical inhalation through habitual laboratorial work, *nor* his familial history with cancer. Subsequently, rather than conduct a *laryngoscopy,* Dr. Goodman prescribes prednisone to treat what he believes to be asthma. *Three months later,* Mr. White returns, complaining that the symptoms have worsened. Accordingly, Dr. Goodman performs a *laryngoscopy,* takes a biopsy, and sends the tissue sample to a laboratory for testing. Thereafter, it is determined that Mr. White has *laryngeal cancer,* which has proven — after a CT scan — to have spread to his lymph nodes. *Furiously,* Mr. White brings a claim for medical negligence against his doctor, though dies shortly thereafter. Appreciably, it is shown, at the time of the initial misdiagnosis Mr. White had a 40% chance of survival, which by the time of a correct diagnosis, declined to 10%.

This is the *archetypal* circumstance where the loss of chance doctrine would arguably apply as an exception, *i.e., a reasonable alternative to the default "but for" test,* allowing proportionate recovery for denial of a better outcome. Currently, this approach is precluded from application in a number of jurisdictions.[71]

---

[70] *See e.g.,* Acharya, *supra* note 30; Weinrib, *supra* note 28, at 157-64; Luntz, *supra* note 4; Sonny Bal & Lawrence H. Brenner, *Medicolegal Sidebar: The Law and Social Values: Loss of Chance,* 472 Clin. Ortho. & Related Rsch. 2923 (2014); and Yu, *supra* note 29, at 45 ("Chinese courts are so flexible that they may apply either proportional liability or the lost chance doctrine to medical cases involving causal uncertainty at their discretion.").
[71] 2003 CanLII 50091; Acharya, *supra* note 30; Luntz, *supra* note 4; Erdman, *supra* note 26, at 315; and Solomon, *supra* note 17, at 618.

THE MODERN STATE OF THE LOSS OF CHANCE DOCTRINE

The most efficient and useful way of understanding the modern state of *the loss of chance doctrine* in cases of medical negligence is by exploring its evolution, *vis-à-vis* examining the whole through the sum of its parts, and how it has been applied globally.

OH CANADA!

Canadian courts have taken the opposite course to *Chaplin v. Hicks,* [1911] 2 K.B. 786 when considering application of this loss of chance doctrine — *specifically as to medical negligence.*

In 1991, the Supreme Court of Canada contemplated application of this doctrine in *Laferrière v. Lawson,* 1991 CanLII 87 (SCC), a case involving a doctor's failure to inform the patient of her cancer.[72] In *Laferrière,* the patient's excised mass was revealed to be cancerous, yet of this, she was failed to be informed. Any additional treatment was not discussed. Consequently, it was only when the patient's health declined that her previous diagnosis was revealed to her. Subsequently, treatment commenced, *however,* the patient passed before the legal proceedings she had initiated had concluded. Ultimately, *Laferrière* was dismissed on its merits, but surprisingly was later overturned by the Quebec Court of Appeal, with a majority finding in favor of the patient. On further appeal, the Supreme Court of Canada had the opportunity to clarify, "whether an action can succeed even where it is not proven that the patient's fate would have been different absent the doctor's fault."[73] *Rephrased,* this Court was tasked with determining, specific to Quebec civil law, whether the loss

---

[72] [1991] 1 SCR 541.
[73] *Id.*

of chance doctrine ought to be applicable in matters concerning medical responsibility.

Notably, the Supreme Court of Canada began its analysis by exploring the application of the loss of chance doctrine in both France and Belgium, pointing to both countries' stark criticism of this doctrine as it pertains to the medical negligence context. Specifically, speaking on behalf of the majority, Justice Gonthier cites that in the medical context, the greatest opposition arises in Belgium and France when the doctrine is applied to circumstances where the patient's chance has already been exhausted.[74] However, even in light of such opposition, Justice Gonthier found this doctrine has still been applied. Particularly, in these countries, "it is the chance itself which is considered," and therefore, damages are partially awarded.[75] Appreciably, this is in contrast to Quebec, where in medical negligence, loss of chance analysis has largely been confined to the actual damage, irrespective of the chance itself.

In fact, Quebec courts seek to employ the loss of chance doctrine only where it can be shown that the plaintiff has established on *the balance of probabilities* (*equiv. preponderance of the evidence*) a causal link between the negligence and the actual damage that manifested. Thus, ineluctably, in Quebec's utilization of this doctrine, it is the "outcome" that is central and the lost chance will only be one part of the analysis.[76]

Interestingly, in concluding, Justice Gonthier held "the judge's duty is to assess the damage suffered by a particular patient, not to remain paraly[z]ed by statistical abstraction."[77] Further, it was held, *the loss of chance doctrine*, as applied in France and Belgium, was not to be introduced in Quebec medical cases. Additionally, Justice Gonthier found no persuasive evidence relative to loss of chance in his review of the jurisprudential positions of the United States and the

---

[74] *Id.*
[75] *Id.*
[76] *Id.*
[77] *Id.*

United Kingdom. *Ergo*, the focus is to be on the concrete benefit denied by negligence, and not the chance of survival.

Thereafter, the Court went on to award damages for psychological suffering and compensation for deprivation of both real and probable improvement, *in terms of quality of life*. Thus, while the plaintiff's death was said not to have been caused by the defendant, the benefit from earlier treatment that she was denied was compensable.[78] Notably, this would not be the last time Justice Gonthier dealt with the loss of chance doctrine in a matter before the Supreme Court of Canada.

ANOTHER STAB, SHALL WE?

In 2002 the loss of chance doctrine was addressed once more by Justice Gonthier in the Supreme Court of Canada's hearing of *St-Jean v. Mercier*, [2002] 1 SCR 491.[79] Specifically, the surgeon, *in this case*, failed to conduct proper testing of a patient presenting with open leg fractures and head bleeding. *He as well*, failed to immobilize the patient for spinal stabilization. Consequently, the patient suffered paraparesis.

Justice Gonthier, *speaking on behalf of the Majority*, held the lost chance failed to be adequate to prove the surgeon's negligence had resulted in paraparesis. Why? Essentially, the original harm causing the patient to attend the hospital offset any negative impact possibly accruing from the surgeon's poor treatment. Thus, Justice Gonthier went on to reaffirm what he deemed "the traditional principle" established in *Laferrière*, stating: "causation must be established on a balance of probabilities and that the loss of a mere chance cannot be a compensable harm"— a statement which was further affirmed just one year later in *Cottrelle v. Gerrard*, 2003 CanLII 50091 (ON CA).[80]

---

[78] *Id.;* and Luntz, *supra* note 4.
[79] *St-Jean v. Mercier*, [2002] 1 SCR 491; and Luntz, *supra* note 4.
[80] *Id.*

A WINDOW OF OPPORTUNITY

In *Cottrelle*, the patient, a diabetic, complained to her doctor of a sore in-between her toes.[81] However, the doctor failed to examine the patient's foot, which later became gangrenous, resulting in amputation of her leg. At trial, medical experts from both sides testified that had the sore been earlier treated, amputation might not have been necessary. Nevertheless, the patient's diabetic condition prevented any expert from suggesting — *with certainty* — the leg would have been saved. Astonishingly, this did not prevent the trial judge from finding that the doctor's negligence deprived the patient a "window of opportunity" to avoid amputation.[82] Necessarily, such deprivation was sufficient to impose liability and award damages.

On appeal, the Ontario Court of Appeal held that the trial judge erred, as evidence substantiating the avoidance of an outcome through proper diagnosis is insufficient in so far as avoidance was not *more than likely*. Accordingly, Justice Sharpe, *for the majority*, found no evidence had been presented which would meet the threshold required in establishing causation. Rather, there was clear evidence indicating irrespective of any negligence, amputation was *more than likely* to have occurred. Consequently, Justice Sharpe reaffirmed that loss of chance is neither applicable nor compensable in medical malpractice cases, unless the chance lost exceeds 50%. Thus, although the patient had shown a "real" lost chance, the percentage of said chance was insufficient in grounding liability.[83]

Interestingly, in *Cottrelle*, Justice Sharpe acknowledges the criticism that has been directed toward the preclusion of the loss of chance doctrine in the medical context. However, he notes that remuneration under this doctrine "would require substantial reduction of the damages to reflect the value of the less than 50 percent chance that was lost."[84] *Ergo*, even if such awards were possible, Justice

---

[81] 2003 CanLII 50091; and Luntz, *supra* note 4.
[82] *Id.*
[83] *Id.*
[84] *Id.*

Sharpe cites *Laferrière* and *St-Jean*, amongst other authorities, which explicitly prohibit such entertainment. As such, *Laferrière* is binding in Ontario, and *Cottrelle* has been followed since then by a number of cases.[85]

    Apropos, in Canada for a patient to succeed in a case where a physician's negligence resulted in a lost chance in achieving a better outcome, it must be established that such loss exceeded the 50% threshold required for satisfying causation on a *balance of probabilities* (*equiv. preponderance of the evidence*).[86]

---

[85] *Id.*

[86] *Id.*; Acharya, *supra* note 30; Erdman, *supra* note 71; and Solomon, *supra* note 71.

THE UNITED KINGDOM – MISCHIEF MANAGED

Two important cases, with which this doctrine has been grappled in the United Kingdom, are *Hotson v. East Berkshire Health Auth.*, [1987] 2 All ER 909 and *Gregg v. Scott*, [2005] UKHL 2. Appreciably, the decisions stemming from these two seminal cases did not have the effect of burying the loss of chance doctrine.[87] However, Harold Luntz, *who is recognized as a leading authority in the area of torts*, has suggested most see the loss of chance doctrine as "no longer open to the courts to apply."[88]

In *Hotson*, the patient sued for negligent misdiagnosis of an acute traumatic fracture of his left femoral epiphysis.[89] Specifically, the patient fell from a tree, resulting in the injury sustained, *however*, a hospital staff member failed to make the correct diagnosis and elected to discharge the patient. *Sometime later*, the patient returned to the hospital in great pain, and this time, was correctly diagnosed. Ultimately, the patient suffered a permanent loss in the form of avascular necrosis of his epiphysis.

---

[87] *Hotson v. E. Berkshire Health Auth.*, [1987] 2 All ER 909; *Gregg v. Scott*, [2005] UKHL 2; and Luntz, *supra* note 4.

[88] Luntz, *supra* note 4.

[89] *Id.*; and [1987] 2 All ER 909.

Notably, the Hospital admitted negligence concerning the misdiagnosis. However, at trial it was held the patient, due to his accident alone, had a 75% chance of developing the relevant loss. Necessarily, the House of Lords sought to treat this probability as a matter of **past fact** with a percentage indicative of certainty, which precluded a finding that any chance was in fact lost.[90] As previously mentioned, the House of Lords left application of the loss of chance doctrine expressly open, stating the following:

> "[U]nless and until this House departs from the decision in *McGhee* your Lordships cannot affirm the proposition that in no circumstances can evidence of a loss of a chance resulting from the breach of a duty of care found a successful claim of damages."[91]

MISSED IT BY THAT MUCH

Similarly, in *Gregg v. Scott,* the House of Lords was presented with a case of physician misdiagnosis, in which it had to be determined whether recovery should be permitted where chance of survival was beneath the 50% threshold.[92] Specifically, the patient's malignant cancer was misdiagnosed, resulting in delayed treatment — reducing the chance of survival from 42% to 25%. At trial, both dissenting Lords Nicholls and Hope argued in favor of application of the loss of chance doctrine. Particularly, Lord Nicholls of Birkenhead argued strongly against a state of the law in which patients who had been denied a real chance at a better outcome could go unprotected by the courts, *stating*:

> This surely cannot be the state of the law today. It would be irrational and indefensible. The loss of a 45% prospect of recovery is just as much a real loss for a patient as the loss of a 55% prospect of recovery... But, it is said, in one case the patient has a remedy, in the other he does not.[93]

---

[90] *Id.*
[91] *Id.*
[92] [2005] UKHL 2; and Luntz, *supra* note 4.
[93] [2005] UKHL 2.

Unfortunately, a narrow majority did not take this view, precluding the patient from recovery. Baroness Hale further added, it is the sheer complexity, of which, is often involved when applying this doctrine in cases of medical malpractice, thus, she suggests "it should not be done."[94]

Consequently, as stated previously, though *Hotson* and *Gregg* did not have the effect of utterly renouncing the loss of chance doctrine, the effect was very likely achieved none the less. Accordingly, having now examined Canada and the United Kingdom, two countries that have rejected the loss of chance doctrine, we now shift in the next section to explore how Australia has *likewise* contended with loss of chance.

---

[94] *Id.*

Chapter 8

AN UNREQUITED LOVE
FROM THE LAND DOWN UNDER

In line with the title of this chapter, Australia has rejected the application of the loss of chance doctrine in cases of medical malpractice.[95] Necessarily, nowhere is this better outlined than in the seminal High Court of Australia case *Tabet v. Gett*, [2010] HCA 12, 240 CLR 537, where a unanimous court saw fit to reject this doctrine's utilization.[96]

Specifically, Tabet had experienced headaches, nausea, and vomiting prior to, *and following*, her recent development of chickenpox. Accordingly, these were the symptoms for which she was admitted to the hospital. Thereafter, Dr. Gett offered a *provisional diagnosis* of chickenpox, meningitis, or encephalitis. However, just three days later, Tabet experienced a seizure and was subsequently diagnosed with a brain tumor (which had developed over a *two-year plus* period). Consequently, Tabet sustained permanent brain damage stemming from the seizure, the presence of the tumor, and its

---

[95] Luntz, *supra* note 4, at 27 ("With Tabet v Gett Australia has joined those common law jurisdictions which reject the doctrine of loss of chance in medical negligence cases.").
[96] *Tabet v. Gett*, [2010] HCA 12, 240 CLR 537; and Luntz, *supra* note 4.

subsequent excision. Surprisingly, the trial judge applied the loss of chance doctrine in favor of Tabet, *however*, the Court of Appeal overturned this decision, arguing in favor of the *balance of probabilities* (*equiv. preponderance of the evidence*) as the sole criterion in assessing and establishing causation.

Following such ruling, Tabet appealed to the High Court, where the core issue was whether "to reformulate the law of torts to permit recovery for physical injury not shown to be caused or contributed to by a negligent party, but which negligence has deprived the victim of the possibility (but not the probability) of a better outcome."[97]

In addressing this issue, acting Chief Justice Gummow saw no reason why tort law's "causation" ought to be weakened, thereby giving the plaintiff the advantage of discharging an easier burden. Therefore, this Court held that unless the loss of chance is *more probable than not*, recovery is precluded.[98] Notably, contract law's version of loss of chance, as outlined in *Chaplin v. Hicks*, [1911] 2 K.B. 786, could not be imported into the law of torts, as this Court pointed to the following fundamental difference inherent in both areas:

> [I]n a negligence action, unlike an action in contract, the existence and causation of compensable loss cannot be established by reference to breach of an antecedent promise to afford an opportunity.[99]

Appreciably, *as will be shown*, the approaches taken by Canada, the United Kingdom, and Australia — in rejecting the loss of chance doctrine as *comportable* in medical negligence cases — are strikingly different from those of 26 states in the US.[100]

---

[97] [2010] HCA 12.
[98] *Id.*
[99] *Id.*
[100] *See, e.g.,* 452 Mass. 1; 836 N.W.2d 321; 126 N.M. 807; 255 Kan. at 218; 481 Pa. 256; 146 Haw. 540; 828 S.W.2d 681; 393 N.W.2d 131; 691 A.2d 641; 734 N.E.2d 535; 2003 WY 91; 107 Nev. 1; 361 Or. 456; 1987 OK 69; 141 Ariz. 597; 498 So. 2d 713; NH Rev. Stat. § 507-E:2 (2019); *Weymers v. Khera*, 454 Mich. 639, at 653 (1997); Mich. Comp. Laws Ann. §

600.2912a(2) (West); *Crosby v. United States*, 48 F.Supp.2d 924 (D. Alaska 1999); Alaska Stat. § 09.55.540; and *Kemper v. Gordon*, 272 S.W.3d 146, 159 (Ky. 2008).

Chapter 9

UNITED STATES OF AMERICA

Ca. Forty-seven years ago, the application of tort law was widely uniform across the United States, with most courts requiring a causal link to be established on a *preponderance of the evidence* (*equiv. balance of probabilities*).[101] However, in response to a certain *disaffection* with the state of affairs rendered *via* determining requisite causation, a number of states began to work toward (*if not simply entertain*) applying a new mechanism within matters of medical malpractice.[102]

For purposes of explicating this doctrinal shift, it is *necessary* to explore *Matsuyama v. Birnbaum*, 452 Mass. 1 (2008), *abrogated by Doull v. Foster*, 487 Mass. 1 (2021), a seminal case that appreciably provides a broad overview of these changes.[103]

MASSACHUSETTS: "YOU HAD ME AT HELLO"

Specifically, the patient complained of heartburn and difficulty

---

[101] Guest, *supra* note 3; and Luntz, *supra* note 4.

[102] *See, e.g.,* 452 Mass. 1; 836 N.W.2d 321; 126 N.M. 807; 255 Kan. at 218; 481 Pa. 256; 146 Haw. 540; 828 S.W.2d 681; 393 N.W.2d 131; 691 A.2d 641; 734 N.E.2d 535; 2003 WY 91; 107 Nev. 1; 361 Or. 456; 1987 OK 69; 141 Ariz. 597; and 498 So. 2d 713.

[103] 452 Mass. at 26-28; Renehan, *supra* note 38, at 14; and 836 N.W.2d at 335.

for Sam & Renee

breathing. Notably, the physician was aware of the patient's history of smoking and past residency in Korea and Japan, placing him at a "significantly higher risk for developing gastric cancer."[104] *However*, no tests were ordered by the physician, who instead, relied solely on physical examination in both rendering a diagnosis of gastrointestinal reflux and suggesting over the counter medications.

Over the next four years the patient returned complaining of similar symptoms increasing in intensity, finally convincing the physician to proceed with definitive diagnostic tests. A gastric mass spanning two-centimeters was revealed, and a diagnosis of type IV *linitis plastica* in signet ring cell carcinoma was offered. Subsequently, the patient underwent treatment, though passed away shortly thereafter.[105]

At trial, it was determined that at the time of the initial negligent misdiagnosis, the patient's chance of survival was 37.5%. Accordingly, the loss of chance doctrine was applied and *pro rata* damages awarded. Thereafter, on appeal to the Supreme Judicial Court of Massachusetts, the issue for determination was whether the loss of chance doctrine's application was permissible as a means for patient recovery in a medical malpractice suit. In addressing the issue, Chief Justice Marshall asserted that not only does the loss of chance doctrine advance "the fundamental goals and principles" of tort law in Massachusetts, but also ensures that those principles and goals "remain fully applicable to the modern world of sophisticated medical diagnosis and treatment."[106] *In recognition of this*, this Court joined the majority of states in endorsing application of the loss of chance doctrine in medical malpractice cases.[107]

Notably, *in applying this doctrine*, Chief Justice Marshall held, "the crux of liability for loss of chance is that Birnbaum's

---

[104] 452 Mass. at 5.
[105] *Id.*
[106] *Id.* at 10-11.
[107] *Id.*

negligence caused a diminution in Matsuyama's likelihood of achieving a more favorable outcome for his medical condition."[108] Alternatively, it was open to the jury to conclude, "but for Birnbaum's breach of care, Matsuyama's chances of survival would have been greater."[109] *Worth recording*, in assessing damages, this Court affirmed the following calculations are to be done:

(1) What are the full damages?

"[C]alculate the total amount of damages allowable...This is the amount to which the decedent would be entitled if the case were not a loss of chance case..."[110]

(2) What was the patient's chance of survival prior to negligence?

"[T]he patient's chance of survival or cure immediately preceding ("but for") the medical malpractice."[111]

(3) What was the patient's chance of survival after negligence?

"[T]he chance of survival or cure that the patient had as a result of the medical malpractice."[112]

(4) Subtract post-negligence survival from pre-negligence survival

Step 2 – Step 3 = %

(5) Multiply full damages (x) by the percentage amount achieved in Step 4 (y)

$(x)(y)$ = "proportional damages award for loss of chance"[113]

In comparison to the above approach, sixteen states in the US have outwardly rejected the application of this doctrine in the medical negligence context.[114] Appreciably, *Kemper v. Gordon*, 272 S.W.3d 146, 159 (Ky. 2008) and *Matsuyama*, are two pivotal cases that represent the stark dichotomy observable in United States case law.

---

[108] *Id*. at 30.
[109] *Id*.
[110] *Id*. at 27.
[111] *Id*.
[112] *Id*.
[113] 452 Mass. at 26-27 ("The most widely adopted of these methods of valuation is the 'proportional damages' approach."); 836 N.W.2d at 335; and 734 N.E.2d at 541.
[114] Guest, *supra* note 3; Fangrow, *supra* note 3; and *see also* Jones, *supra* note 6.

Specifically, as recognized by Tory Weigand in *Lost Chances, Felt Necessities, and the Tale of Two Cities*, 43 Suffolk U.L. Rev. 327 (2010), these two cases, decided within a month of one another, represent two sides of a similar situation.[115] Both involve fatalities from cancer, under circumstances where misdiagnosis occurred, leading to an action for loss of a chance. However, loss of chance was applied in one and not the other.

KENTUCKY: "BEWARE THE IDES OF MARCH"

In *Kemper*, Lori Gordon presented to the hospital experiencing multiple symptoms.[116] At that time, testing produced negative results and she was discharged.[117] Two months later, symptoms resurfaced and she was prescribed Ativan for anxiety.[118] The following day, Lori consulted Dr. Kemper, who prescribed *alprazolam* for anxiety, and when symptoms persisted, he recommended she consult with a psychiatrist.[119] Subsequently, the psychiatrist diagnosed her with anxiety, and prescribed various pharmaceuticals to treat the disorder.[120] With the persistence of symptoms, Lori sought out another internist, *who too*, diagnosed anxiety.[121] After five months — still experiencing symptoms — it was discovered that Lori now had an enlarged lymph node, in addition to a proximal mass.[122] Consequently, Lori received a formal diagnosis of metastasized gastric cancer.[123]

Approximately one year later, Lori passed away in the midst

---

[115] Tory A. Weigand, *Lost Chances, Felt Necessities, and the Tale of Two Cities*, 43 Suffolk U.L. Rev. 327, 327-28 and 381-82 (2010) ("The Kemper and Matsuyama decisions capture the debate over whether medical malpractice liability should be expanded to include responsibility for lost chances of a better outcome, as well as the divergent views as to the appropriate role and limits to judicial power and policymaking as to physician liability.").
[116] *Kemper v. Gordon*, 272 S.W.3d 146, 148 (Ky. 2008).
[117] *Id.*
[118] *Id.*
[119] *Id.*
[120] *Id.*
[121] *Id.*
[122] 272 S.W.3d at 149.
[123] *Id.*

of her multiple negligence claims.[124] Notably, all cases had been decided with the exception of the one brought against Dr. Kemper.[125]

Accordingly, the Supreme Court of Kentucky granted discretionary review to determine whether the Court of Appeal's application of the loss of chance doctrine to this case should be permissible.[126] To that end, this Court answered in the negative, precluding any compensability under loss of chance *above or below* 50%.[127] This Court's reasoning relied heavily on policy, asserting such application would set too high a financial burden on the physicians and the public.[128] Further, the sheer complexity application would entail, and the fact that this doctrine represented a "significant departure from the traditional meaning of causation in tort law" led to its rejection entirely.[129]

As it stands today, 26 states in the United States have adopted the loss of chance doctrine in some form or another, with 16 states conversely rejecting its application. As stated previously, both Kemper and Matsuyama represent the stark dichotomy observable within and across the United States.

---

[124] *Id.*
[125] *Id.*
[126] 272 S.W.3d at 146.
[127] 272 S.W.3d at 148.
[128] 272 S.W.3d at 152 ("We are troubled by the potential financial burden that might be spread upon the shoulders of millions of people if we adopt this new concept of lost or diminished chance of recovery.").
[129] 272 S.W.3d at 152-53 (citing *Smith v. Parrott*, 2003 VT 64, 175 Vt. 375, 833 A.2d 843, 848 (2003)).

THE LOSS OF CHANCE DOCTRINE'S APPLICATION
ACROSS THE UNITED STATES OF AMERICA

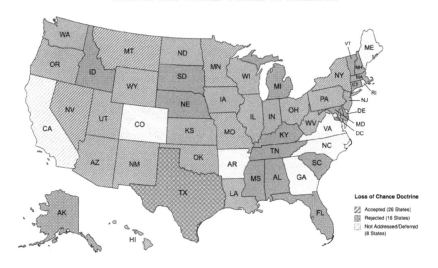

This geographical representation was created by Matthew Walker by compiling stats from the requisite sources.[130]

[130] Guest, *supra* note 3; Fangrow, *supra* note 3; and *see also* Jones, *supra* note 6; 452 Mass. 1; 836 N.W.2d 321; 126 N.M. 807; 255 Kan. at 218; 481 Pa. 256; 146 Haw. 540; 828 S.W.2d 681; 393 N.W.2d 131; 691 A.2d 641; 734 N.E.2d 535; 2003 WY 91; 107 Nev. 1; 361 Or. 456; 1987 OK 69; 141 Ariz. 597; 498 So. 2d 713; NH Rev. Stat. § 507-E:2 (2019); 454 Mich. 639, at 653 (1997); Mich. Comp. Laws Ann. § 600.2912a(2) (West); 48 F.Supp.2d 924 (D. Alaska 1999); Alaska Stat. § 09.55.540; and 272 S.W.3d 146, 159 (Ky. 2008).

EXERCISE: A RELATIVE ANALYSIS IN PLACE OF A THRESHOLD ONE
Possible Solutions to Bring Balance to Tort — at this point, having just discussed two pivotal decisions in the United States, *with differing outcomes*, I now take the *proportional damages approach* and offer two possible variants. Notably, the first and second variants, *the traditional doctrine+* and *pro rata extremus* respectively, represent a combination of the approaches taken in *Matsuyama* and the dissent in *Kemper*.[131] Upon reviewing these variants, try and see if either could provide a requisite mechanism for compensation that fits within the current framework of tort law across a number of jurisdictions. Keep in mind, the goal is to resolve the causal uncertainty which ever so frequently burdens medical negligence actions.
THE CALCULATION
Necessarily, in both of these variants, the requisite calculations are to be done in ascertaining *pro rata* damages for loss of chance: **(1) What are the full damages?** The full amount to which the plaintiff would be entitled, had "but for" causation been satisfied. **(2) What was the patient's chance of survival or recovery prior to negligence?** *Added by the Author** patient specific statistical analysis: the court must look at average survival rate distribution and determine where the patient fell on it (looking at patient specific factors).[132] **(3) What was the patient's chance of survival after negligence?** "[T]he chance of survival or cure that the patient had as a result of the medical malpractice."[133] **(4) Subtract post-negligence survival from pre-negligence survival** *Step 2 – Step 3 = %* **(5) Multiply full damages (x) by the percentage amount achieved in Step 4 (y)** *(x)(y)* = "proportional damages award for loss of chance"[134]
Recall, this calculation is characterized as the *proportional damages approach* adopted in *Matsuyama*.[135] However, in line with the dissent's reasoning in *Kemper*, this approach would not be precluded from application where the outcome has not yet manifested.[136] This follows, as "the injury is the loss of opportunity for a better result."[137] Having established the requisite calculation, we may now explore the two variants, beginning with *the traditional doctrine+*

---

[131] 452 Mass. at 26-28; and 272 S.W.3d at 161.

[132] *See* Gould, *supra* note 1.

[133] 452 Mass. at 27.

[134] 452 Mass. at 26-27; 836 N.W.2d at 335; and 734 N.E.2d at 541

[135] 452 Mass. at 26 ("The most widely adopted of these methods of valuation is the 'proportional damages' approach."); 836 N.W.2d at 335; and *Cahoon v. Cummings*, 734 N.E.2d 535, 541 (Ind. 2000).

[136] 272 S.W.3d at 161.

[137] 272 S.W.3d at 159.

A. THE TRADITIONAL DOCTRINE +

My first variant of the loss of chance doctrine, only *varies* from the typical doctrine applied in *Matsuyama* to the extent that it includes an *add-on*. Specifically, the 50% principle remains in place, offering patients full recovery where the chance lost surpasses this threshold. Consequently, where the chance lost sits beneath this threshold, full recovery is precluded, however, *proportionate recovery* is permissible. The calculation above is applied, with justification stemming from the principles and reasoning outlined by the majority in *Matsuyama* and the dissent in *Kemper*.[138] Notice, ***the only difference*** here is that the court must examine *patient-specific factors* in determining the patient's chance of survival or recovery prior to negligence.[139] Why is this a good thing? What factors ought to be considered by courts? Is such an exercise to onerous and complex?

B. PRO RATA EXTREMUS

My second variant of the loss of chance doctrine relies more heavily on the reasoning set out by the dissent in *Kemper*, by which a *proportionate damages approach*, "would result in more verdicts, but those would be balanced by lower damage awards."[140] Fundamentally, the calculation from *Matsuyama* is applied exactly as presented above, with the only change being the removal of the 50% threshold. Therefore, full recovery would only be permitted in the rarest of occasions with a significant majority of awards being proportional to the chance lost. Under this approach physicians would rarely (*if ever*) pay full damages, and plaintiffs would likely be able to recover more frequently. In line with the dissent in *Kemper*, if such an approach were adopted, it would seem inappropriate to argue that courts would be overburdened by "unnecessary litigation."[141] Such an assumption is completely unfounded and unsubstantiated.[142] Are full damages a good thing? Can you think of a case where full recovery ought to be awarded? What issues might arise with an approach like this?

It is important to keep in mind that a number of jurisdictions have rejected the loss of chance doctrine, *and therefore*, I essentially offer the proportionate damages approach, *with my add-on and alteration*, simply as one mechanism (*with variants*) through which other jurisdictions might apply the loss of chance doctrine. To see a more comprehensive and balanced approach, review *the Walker Approach* presented later on.

---

[138] 452 Mass. at 26-28; and 272 S.W.3d at 161.

[139] *See* Gould, *supra* note 1. One might argue there are other factors of relevance beyond for instance those considered in staging based on TNM. *See* 452 Mass. at 8–9, stating:
> Finkel offered an extensive discussion of the tumor-lymph nodes-metastasis (TNM) method for classifying gastric cancer into separate "stages,".... Patients with stage 0, in which the cancer is confined to the stomach lining, have a better than 90% survival rate, Finkel averred; at stage 1, the survival rate drops to between 60% and 80%; at stage 2, between 30% and 50%; at stage 3, between 10% and 20%; and at stage 4, less than 4%.17 Finkel opined that, as a result of Birnbaum's breach of the standard of care, Matsuyama lost the opportunity of having gastric cancer "diagnosed and treated in a timely fashion when it might still have been curable."

[140] 272 S.W.3d at 161.

[141] *Id.*

[142] *See e.g.*, 836 N.W.2d at 349 n. 14.

Chapter 10

A SPOON FULL OF SUGAR

OR

A SHOCK TO THE SYSTEM?

Should We Apply the Loss of Chance Doctrine in Medical Negligence Cases? There are *two voices* which *I feel* can be discerned from the prodigious amount of literature pertaining to this doctrine. These two voices comprise views which sit directly opposite on a spectrum. Specifically, Professor Ernest Weinrib (*Professor Emeritus, University of Toronto, Faculty of Law*) argues in favor of applying the loss of chance doctrine, while Professor Nayha Acharya (*Assistant Professor of Law, Schulich School of Law, Dalhousie University*) directly opposes such application. *Apropos*, I propose to outline these two positions in this section, and thereafter, offer my analysis.

ERNEST WEINRIB'S TWO "ORACULAR" POSSIBILITIES

Professor Weinrib offers the latest of proposals directed toward the application of the *loss of chance doctrine* in cases of medical malpractice.[143] Professor Weinrib suggests, the issue boils down to the fact that these types of negligence cases often involve a patient who

---

[143] Acharya, *supra* note 30, at 207.

might have succumbed to their condition even in the face of earlier treatment.[144] This results in a difficult balancing act:

> "[O]n the one hand, the defendant has breached a duty of care... On the other hand, under the "but for" test the defendant's negligence seems not to have been a factual cause of the plaintiff's ultimate harm."[145]

Importantly, Weinrib states that although the patient is at a risk, the genesis of such risk is not associated in any way with the physician.[146] However, the physician's culpability could be realized instead in the denial of avoiding such risk through the physician's own negligence.[147] Under this approach, liability might be imposed and damages awarded *pro rata*.[148] Weinrib provides the following illustration:

> "A plaintiff whom the defendant's negligence deprived of a 30 per cent chance of recovery would be awarded 30 per cent of the damages that would have been awarded for the ultimate harm had factual causation been provable.[149]

According to Weinrib, this approach affords the system of tort law a mechanism for redress, compensating the patient for this diminution.[150] As well, it ensures our law recognizes physician negligence which denies a patient realization of "the already slim chance."[151]

How the relationship between compensation for the chance that was lost and the right which was infringed upon is understood, determines whether this doctrine is viewed as in accord with our law on negligence.[152]

---

[144] Weinrib, *supra* note 28, at 139.
[145] *Id.* at 157.
[146] *Id.*
[147] *Id.*
[148] *Id.*
[149] *Id.* at 158.
[150] *Id.*
[151] *Id.*
[152] *Id.*

Weinrib offers two such possibilities for conceptualizing loss of chance, as either constituting:

I. "the infringement of an independent right to the enjoyment of that chance;" _or_

II. "the injury to the plaintiff's right to have the defendant act in a particular way."[153]

This first conceptualization envisions the chance itself as an independent right. As this conceptualization is, _as acknowledged by Weinrib_, burdened with several issues, I will only detail the second conceptualization, which Weinrib contends to be the more plausible and less problematic of the two.[154]

This second conceptualization focuses on the patient's right to have the physician perform in a way, consistent with that expected of a competent medical practitioner. According to Weinrib, the chance at recovery "is an incident of this right."[155] Thus, when chance suffers wrongful diminution, it becomes a descriptive "tool", indicating how the right to proper and competent care was injured. Further, Weinrib suggests this "tool" additionally offers a measure for the valuation of damages, _via_ probabilistic expression of chance.

This conceptualization is not inherently different from how loss of chance operates within contract law. In support of this, Weinrib offers a comparison to _Chaplin v. Hicks,_ [1911] 2 K.B. 786, a case argued inapplicable in the context of medical negligence, and a case which I have already detailed herein.[156] To resolve this inapplicability, Weinrib suggests that we consider the patient's right, in the medical context, as _in personam_, a right acquired through a given interaction.[157] Essentially, through the patient's reliance on the physician's treatments and diagnoses, a right to be treated competently arises.[158] _Ipso facto_, the physician undertakes treatment

---

[153] _Id._
[154] _Id._ at 160.
[155] _Id._
[156] _Id._
[157] _Id._ at 161-63.
[158] _Id._

of the patient, for which the patient forgoes seeking treatment elsewhere in reliance of the former's treatment offering a chance for recovery.[159]

Accordingly, the injury suffered is not the final outcome of death, disability, *etc.*, but rather, it is both the denial of chance and the occurrence of the final outcome which ground liability. *With that*, Weinrib postulates, "the probability of the chance's materializing is the measure of the defendant's compensation for its loss."[160]

Necessarily, this conceptualization avoids the pitfalls Professor Weinrib identified in the first conceptualization previously offered, as (1) the scope is confined to the loss suffered through reliance; (2) where factual causation is shown, the plaintiff is not confined to *pro rata* damages; and (3) liability is not imposed where the detriment has not been suffered in combination with the lost chance.[161] In line with this last point, this conceptualization would not allow for recovery where the outcome has not materialized.[162]

NAYHA ACHARYA'S AFFINITY FOR COHERENCY AND INTEGRITY

Comparably, Assistant Professor Nayha Acharya offers a direct counter to Professor Weinrib's proposal. Essentially, Acharya's encapsulating argument is that the results across all categories of torts would be inconsistent if the loss of chance doctrine were to apply solely in the context of medical negligence.[163]

Ultimately, it is Acharya's belief that the application of this doctrine, as confined to a single category of tort, "opens a gate for the arbitrary, illegitimate exercise of legal authority."[164] Accordingly, she points to "the value of coherence through consistency" within tort law as the key element through which our "adjudicative system" derives its fairness.[165]

---

[159] *Id.*
[160] *Id.* at 163.
[161] *Id.*
[162] *Id.*
[163] Acharya, *supra* note 30, at 221-24.
[164] *Id.* at 223.
[165] *Id.* at 222-23.

Necessarily, *to appreciate her predication better*, Acharya offers the following "analogous" scenario, which rather than paraphrase, is offered here below for added value to your review:

> Suppose a university is endowed with funds and must decide how to distribute them through scholarships. The awards can be justified in several ways, such as academic merit, financial need, or in furtherance of some societal welfare goal. The University must choose how to justify the awards. The chosen justification will then be embedded into the policy that the university settles on. Suppose the university decides that the scholarship will be awarded solely on the basis of academic achievement. That justification (i.e. academic merit) is then embedded into the policy. The policy must be applied consistently, even though other justifications exist (like social welfare concerns or financial need). It would be improper to give an individual the scholarship based on financial need, because financial need is not the justification that underpins that scholarship. Although it may seem to be a laudable outcome, the decision to make that award would be incoherent, arbitrary, and unfair.[166]

Appreciably, *pursuant to this scenario*, Acharya claims that it comparably would be "inappropriate" to introduce the loss of chance doctrine in handling causal uncertainty; thereby, providing (*affording*) *pro rata* recovery.[167] **Why?** According to Acharya, both treatment and decisions rendered across all tort cases would be unjustifiably incoherent, threatening the consistency and coherency which are central to "the fairness and legitimacy of tort adjudication."[168] Yet, *she as well contends*, "a fulsome articulation of the underpinning values of consistency and coherence in tort law is lacking."[169]

---

[166] *Id.* at 223.

[167] *Id.* ("In the same way, accommodating factual uncertainty by resorting to the loss of chance doctrine may appear desirable because it would afford an injured individual some compensation, but such piecemeal justification is inappropriate.").

[168] *Id.*

[169] *Id.* at 214.

ANALYSIS

Appreciably, *in general*, it could be argued that nullification of the loss of chance doctrine based solely on maintaining *consistency* and *coherency* is concerning, *or at the very least unsatisfactory*, as these values have yet to receive "a fulsome articulation" in tort.[170] Necessarily, Professor Weinrib arguably offers an appealing proposal by which the plaintiff can recover full damages where "but for" causation is established, *and where it is not*, they are afforded the opportunity for *pro rata* recovery. Additionally, Weinrib's proposal *prima facie* limits the scope so that liability is limited where detrimental reliance in combination with loss of a chance is shown. However, I take issue with this proposal's failure to allow recovery for plaintiffs whose adverse outcome has not yet been suffered — *as lost chance constitutes an injury in itself*; and this will be addressed in my analysis of Professor Acharya's arguments.

First, Professor Acharya's assertion that Professor Weinrib's proposal fails to extend to a physician "providing diagnostic or investigative procedures" appears flawed.[171] *Verbatim*, Acharya contends, "[a]t the diagnostic stage, there is no undertaking to provide treatment," and thus, misdiagnosis fails to be compensable.[172]

Consequently, a radiologist would not be held liable for failing to properly examine an *x-ray*, as according to Professor Acharya, "the specialist has in fact *not* undertaken to improve the chances of survival at all."[173]

---

[170] *Id.* at 214.
[171] *Id.* at 218-19.
[172] *Id.* at 218-19.
[173] *Id.* at 219 ("Suppose...a patient is sent to a specialist for a chest x-ray. That specialist negligently misreads the x-ray and assures the patient's physician that she has a benign condition that requires no treatment. As a result of the misdiagnosis, the specialist has in fact not undertaken to improve the chances of survival at all.").

However, the College of Physicians and Surgeons of Ontario (CPSO), defines 'treatment', in line with s.2(1) of the *Health Care Consent Act* as,

> "Anything that is done for a therapeutic, preventable, palliative, diagnostic, cosmetic, or other health-related purpose, and includes a course of treatment, plane of treatment, or community treatment plan."[174]

Ipso facto, not only does the diagnostic stage constitute an undertaking to provide treatment, but contrary to Professor Acharya's belief, a radiologist could be held liable for the negligent misdiagnosis. Considerably, that was exactly the result in *Coody v. Barraza*, 111 So. 3d 485 (2013), where the Louisiana Court of Appeal held a radiologist liable for the loss of chance resulting from his failure to identify and report a *1.5 cm x 2 cm* soft tissue density.[175]

Understandably, the benefit of the loss of chance doctrine is its ability to provide proportionate recovery for a plaintiff who is unable to establish causation *via* the "but for" test. *Ergo*, Professor Acharya's assertion that *pro rata* recovery is irreconcilable with full recovery — the latter of which is awarded where "but for" causation is established — *seems flawed*. This conclusion necessarily follows from the fact that loss of chance is designed to provide "some" compensation for a plaintiff, who otherwise, *under the default law*, is entitled to none. Yet, Acharya argues that where one plaintiff can establish causation, and the other only loss of chance, the "different outcomes for both parties could not be justified."[176]

Conversely, I argue *pro rata* recovery is a *more* justifiable outcome then is currently being offered to plaintiffs unable to establish "but for" causation. However, I completely agree with

---

[174] *See* Consent to Treatment, College of Physicians and Surgeons of Ontario (2001), http://www.cpso.on.ca/Physicians/Policies-Guidance/Policies/Consent-to-Treatment - Endnotes; and Health Care Consent Act, SO 1996, c. 2.

[175] *Coody v. Barraza*, 111 So. 3d 485 (2013) (holding that jury was correct in finding that defendant-radiologist's failure to abide by the requisite standard resulted in Ms. Coody suffering a loss of a chance, with respect to her survival or obtaining a better outcome).

[176] Acharya, *supra* note 30, at 220.

Professor Acharya's criticism of the failure of Professor Weinrib's proposal to provide compensation for a patient where the outcome has not yet manifested. Unfortunately, a viable solution in this area has yet to be offered.[177]

Ultimately, throughout Professor Acharya's paper, application of the loss of chance doctrine is argued against by virtue of the inconsistency in judicial outcomes it would cause across tort law if applied only in cases of medical negligence.[178] *However*, fairness through consistency is not justice. It is just consistency. Assuming that simply because one category is part of a larger category of *tort*, all things contained within the *latter* must be the same, is inapt. *Unequivocally*, I assert, as long as all categories operate and remain grounded within the same framework of tort, each can be different in their pursuit of justice.

Further, there is no reason why the loss of chance doctrine cannot be confined solely to operate within medical malpractice litigation. In fact, evidence of such truth can be found in the United States, where the loss of chance doctrine has been accepted by a majority of states.

For instance, five years following the Supreme Court of Missouri's application of this doctrine, a plaintiff attempted to invoke the doctrine outside of the context of medical malpractice.[179] Consequently, the Appellate Court found no difficulty whatsoever in denying the comportability of the doctrine within the matter before it.[180] Necessarily, in the words of Steven R. Koch, "the ability of the Missouri courts to restrict the lost-chance doctrine to medical

---

[177] *Id.* at 224-25.

[178] *Id.* at 205-25.

[179] *Kemp v. Balboa*, 959 S.W.2d 116 (Mo. Ct. App. 1997), *opinion adopted and reinstated after retransfer* (Mar. 2, 1998); and *Wollen v. DePaul Health Ctr.*, 828 S.W.2d 681 (Mo. 1992).

[180] 959 S.W.2d at 119 ("We are unable to conclude that Wollen opened the door to "lost chance of recovery" claims in every tort action in which a plaintiff contends that his physical injuries may have shortened his life...action was not a medical malpractice action."); and Steven R. Koch, *Whose Loss Is It Anyway? Effects of the "Lost-Chance" Doctrine on Civil Litigation and Medical Malpractice Insurance*, 88 N.C. L. Rev. 595, 631-32 (2010).

malpractice cases is indicative of the ease with which other courts are capable of doing the same."[181]

Lastly, it remains questionable as to why the notion of applying the loss of chance doctrine in other areas of tort, beyond medical negligence, is so inacceptable. After all, *if the sneaker fits*, what is wrong with wearing it?

The idea of how the loss of chance doctrine could suitably apply to the areas of **Autonomous Vehicles** and **Nanorobotics**, both emerging markets ripe for liability, is explored in my other soon to be published books that will be available for purchase:

1. Matthew Walker, *Bending Realities: Introducing the Loss of Chance Doctrine into an Automated Multiverse of Madness* (2022); and

2. Matthew Walker, *Nano-Bots, Doctors in Disguise: Exploring Loss of Chance at the Nano-Level* (2022).

Worth noting now, some of the many other arguments that have been proffered by scholars, and the judiciary alike, will be addressed immediately in the next section that follows.

---

[181] Koch, *supra* note 167.

BETTER TO BEAR A LESSER EVIL THAN TO RISK A GREATER IN REMOVING IT

Not surprisingly, many scholars and courts have relied on the type of reasoning promogulated by Professor Acharya. *Ad nauseum*, this narrative seeks to defeat the arguments asserted by those in favor of introducing the loss of chance doctrine within medical malpractice actions. Essentially, scholars and members of the judiciary alike assume the role of the prophetic mystical soothsayer, forewarning and foretelling of the dreadful *"parade of horribles"* that ought follow should one see it fit to enable plaintiffs to "dance around causation."[182]

But, in reality, such "divinations" have necessarily proven folly, only holding success to the extent they invoke "theater of the mind." For instance, the "Flood Gates" argument is a commonality amongst those who have rejected the loss of chance doctrine.

---

[182] *See e.g., Fennell v. S. Maryland Hosp. Ctr., Inc.*, 320 Md. 776, 797, 580 A.2d 206, 217 (1990) ("the majority should not be so quick to adopt the parade of horribles so facilely conjured up by the defense bar. It is not inevitable that "societal costs" (i.e. insurance premiums) would be increased should this approach to damages be applied, or that new floodgates of litigation will open.").

FLOOD GATES

Specifically, these jurisdictions reason that application of the loss of chance doctrine will result in an increase in claims brought against medical professionals, *thereby* "flooding" the courts with plaintiffs seeking to take advantage of a less burdensome standard of law.[183] In reality, this has proven *untrue*.

For example, in the United States, those jurisdictions that have elected to apply the loss of chance doctrine have seen no such substantial increase in the quantity of claims following such implementation. While this conclusion results from a review of data derived from the National Practitioner Data Bank, it arguably provides a valid indicator of whether a spike has resulted following a state's acceptance of the loss of chance doctrine.[184]

Moreover, *of late*, the United Kingdom has seen a drastic rise in medical malpractice actions, resulting in an exponentially and ever-increasingly costly system, *and yet*, the United Kingdom relegated the loss of chance doctrine to obscurity over 16 years ago.[185]

---

[183] *See e.g.*, 272 S.W.3d at 152 and 161 ("A whole new and expensive industry of experts could conceivably be marched through our courts, providing evidence for juries that an MRI misread on Monday, but accurately discerned on Friday, perhaps gives rise to an infinitesimal loss of a chance to recover. Yet, under this doctrine, even a small percentage of the value of a human life could generate substantial recovery and place burdensome costs on healthcare providers. This additional financial load would be passed along to every man, woman, and child in this Commonwealth.").

[184] Steven R. Koch, *Whose Loss Is It Anyway? Effects of the "Lost-Chance" Doctrine on Civil Litigation and Medical Malpractice Insurance*, 88 N.C. L. Rev. 595, at 619-27 (2010) ("While the volatility of claims paid per year is substantial, an analysis of malpractice insurance premium payments in several states that addressed the lost-chance doctrine in the mid-1990s indicates that the economic effect of such an adoption can be nothing more than a proverbial drop in the bucket.").

[185] House of Commons, *NHS litigation reform*, UK Parliament (2022), https://committees.parliament.uk/publications/22039/documents/163739/default/ (last visited Sep. 7, 2022) ("At the same time, the costs of the system have continued to grow at an eye-watering rate… This sum is set to double over the next decade to £4.6 billion, and around a quarter of such costs go not to families but to lawyers. The English NHS spends 2% of its total income on clinical negligence compared to half that level in New Zealand or Sweden.").

INCREASE MALPRACTICE PREMIUMS

Additionally, another argument advanced by the opposition is that adoption of the loss of chance doctrine will too *exponentially* increase the malpractice insurance premium rates of medical professionals.[186] While one can certainly appreciate the severity and significance of such a result, *in reality*, no such connection has been found either.[187]

TOO MANY ERRORS

Yet still, others such as Tory Weigand, have suggested that "[f]rom a purely statistical point of view, the loss of chance doctrine produces more errors than traditional causation/damage principles."[188] *Worth noting*, to advance this argument, the following premise (*33/66 scenario*) was relied on:

33/66 Scenario

Assume a hypothetical group of 99 cancer patients, each of whom would have had a 33 1/3% chance of survival. Each received negligent medical care, and all 99 died. Traditional tort law would deny recovery in all 99 cases because each patient had less than a 50% chance of recovery and the probable cause of death was the pre-existing cancer not the negligence. Statistically, had all 99 received proper treatment, 33 would have lived and 66 would have died; so the traditional rule would have statistically produced 33 errors by denying recovery to all 99. The loss of chance rule would allow all 99 patients to recover, but each would recover 33 1/3% of the

---

[186] 272 S.W.3d at 152 ("We are troubled by the potential financial burden that might be spread upon the shoulders of millions of people if we adopt this new concept of lost or diminished chance of recovery.").

[187] Koch, *supra* note 167, at 626-30 ("various factors other than medical malpractice claims themselves appear to be the driving force behind the malpractice insurance premium rates... a particular state's adoption of the lost-chance doctrine is even more tangentially related to any potential effect that medical malpractice claims may have on malpractice insurance rates. . . .").

[188] Tory A. Weigand, Esq., *Lost Chances, Felt Necessities, and the Tale of Two Cities*, 43 Suffolk U. L. Rev. 327, 374 (2010); and *see also Fennell v. S. Maryland Hosp. Ctr., Inc.*, 320 Md. 776, 789–90, 580 A.2d 206, 213 (1990).

normal value of the case. Again, with proper care 33 patients would have survived. Thus, the 33 patients who statistically would have survived with proper care would receive only one-third of the appropriate recovery, while the 66 patients who died as a result of the pre-existing condition, not the negligence, would be overcompensated by one-third. The loss of chance rule would have produced errors in all 99 cases.[189]

The essence of this scenario is *essentially*, if we apply the loss of chance doctrine, we get more errors than we would under the traditional doctrine, as we may be compensating plaintiffs for whom, even with proper treatment, would have still died. *Id est*, better to bear a lesser evil than to risk one far worser in removing it. While *prima facie*, the logic here seems quite sound, in reality however, this scenario fails to appreciate the application and aims of the loss of chance doctrine, and chiefly, the *fundamental truths* of medical science and rendering judicial judgments.

Recall, the role of the loss of chance doctrine is to afford those *patient-plaintiffs*, who lost a chance at survival or recovery, some form of compensation. Accordingly, for those who are deemed to have had an initial chance of survival above 50%, recovery is awarded in *full*; and for those whose chance of survival fell below 50%, *proportionate compensation* through the loss of chance doctrine is available. Appreciably, *just like the road not taken*, a court can never realistically know more than the evidence that is available before it.

Consequently, of particular importance is how chance is quantified through the testimony of experts. Necessarily, should experts deem chance, as *in this scenario above*, to be 33 1/3% (*i.e., chance of survival*) for all 99 patients, then that is the only value before the court. Notably, that value encapsulates the initial chance of survival if afforded proper treatment. Yet, this scenario reveals error *via* the fact that in such a case, *even with that 33 1/3% chance*, in reality, 33 would have lived, whilst 66 of those patients would have died. In advancing such a scenario, one is led to observe both the *over-*

---

[189] 320 Md. at 789–90, 580 A.2d at 213 (1990).

compensatory and *under-compensatory* effects, should one adopt the loss of chance doctrine. However, such reality <u>as presented</u>, is utterly incommensurable with that of either medical or judicial reality.

This follows, as one can never truly know whether a given *patient-plaintiff* would have lived or died. And to suggest that courts ought to be frightened of such a fact, fails to appreciate the reality in which negligence and the world operates.[190] In fact, aside from this hypothetical, I have yet to come across a case wherein which a *patient-plaintiff's* survival can be professed to the level of exact certitude that this scenario portends. Necessarily, such *absolutism* may seldom be found within the realities of today's healthcare industry, wherein which <u>chance, *not certainty*</u>, is the requisite currency giving life and weight to each course taken (*and not taken*).

UNWARRANTED DISSUASION

Appreciably, this scenario (*33/66 scenario*) once again speaks to the fear appeals *advanced* and *relied* on by those who seek to relegate the loss of chance doctrine into *nihility*. In other words, this scenario dissuades a jurisdiction's adoption of this doctrine based on the premise that courts may end up awarding more damages than should be owed. But therein lies the crux of uncertainty in negligence, in that one can only ever present the best evidence they have, with decisions rendered based on reasoned judgment, *not exact certainty*.[191]

Noticeably, such jurisdictional dissuasion to adoption of the loss of chance doctrine is achieved *herein (33/66 scenario)* through mere *statistical manipulation* and *selection bias*. *To substantiate this*, one may offer the exact same scenario, but modify the facts so as to include the following statistics:

---

[190] 452 Mass. at 29 ("As we have noted, probabilistic evidence, in the form of actuarial tables, assumptions about present value and future interest rates, statistical measures of future harm, and the like, is the stock-in-trade of tort valuation.").

[191] 452 Mass. at 29 ("For decades, judges, lawyers, jurors, and litigants have shown themselves competent to sift through such evidence in a variety of contexts, from mass toxic torts to single-car collisions.").

Assume each of the 99 cancer patients would have had an initial 99% chance of survival, but all 99 died due to negligent medical care. Under the *all-or-nothing rule* (*i.e.*, *traditional rule*) full recovery would be awarded in all 99 cases. Why? Because each patient had an initial chance surpassing 50%, suggesting that the probable cause of death was the negligence, not cancer. Yet, "statistically," even if each of the 99 patients received proper treatment, none of them would have lived (99 would have died). Thus, the *all-or-nothing rule* (*i.e.*, *traditional rule*) would have statistically produced 99 errors, overcompensating 99 patients.

Indubitably, the scenario I offer above is just one of many that reveals the ease with which the number of errors may be manipulated and presented. This is problematic, as the court in *Fennell v. Southern Maryland Hosp.*, 580 A.2d 206 (Md. 1990) relied on this hypothetical scenario, as one of the reasons for its rejection of the loss of chance doctrine.[192] And in turn, Tory Weigand relied on this sole case, *Fennell*, to advance the argument that the loss of chance doctrine produces more errors than the traditional rule does.[193] Unapologetically, most scholars with an appreciation of, *at the very least*, the Scientific Method, would be *flabbergasted* to see such weight be given to the scenario above. *Ceteris paribus*, this is congruence bias at its best.

---

[192] *Fennell v. S. Maryland Hosp. Ctr., Inc.*, 320 Md. 776, 789–90, 580 A.2d 206, 213 (1990)
[193] Tory A. Weigand, *Lost Chances, Felt Necessities, and the Tale of Two Cities*, 43 Suffolk U. L. Rev. 327, 374 (2010).

THE MYTH OF EARLY DETECTION

We have failed to recognize that most important chronic diseases evolve over decades in a person's body. By the time they come to medical attention, they are well entrenched and not subject to cure. Treatment may alleviate some of the suffering from these conditions, but may also cause problems that harm our overall level of well being… [I]t is commonly believed that bad health outcomes usually result from failure to detect disease early. Certainly, this is true in some cases. Yet, in other cases early detection is of little value. For example, early detection of a disease that will not eventually result in death, disability, or symptoms may be of little importance. Similarly, detection of a disease for which there is no effective treatment cannot lead to a remedy that will make the patient better.[194]

"[E]arly" detection is biologically late"[195] — according to Tory Weigand, one ought to reject the loss of chance doctrine, as early detection and treatment does not always *equate* to a positive outcome, and may even result in harm, not betterment.[196] While in the abstract, such pronouncements may be deemed true, *in reality*, they miss the mark. This follows, as such arguments concerning the *fallibility* of early detection fall short when it comes to (1) those cases concerning loss of chance and (2) those matters wherein which *early detection* would produce statistically viable results.

Beginning with the former, recall, the *modus operandi* of the loss of chance doctrine is quite clear-cut, with recovery being afforded to those *patient-plaintiffs* whose initial chance of recovery fell below 50%. *Ipso facto*, if early detection always resulted in survival or recovery, then there would be no need for loss of chance adoption in jurisdictions. In other words, the loss of chance doctrine is being applied because medical experts at trial have testified that the patient-

---

[194]*Id.* at 366 (*citing* Robert Kaplan, *Disease, Diagnosis, & Dollars* 4 & 35 (2009)).
[195] *Id.* at 366.
[196] *Id.* at 365-70.

plaintiff's chance of survival <u>with proper treatment</u> fell below 50%.[197] *Consequently*, Weigand's argument seems illogical, as the premise it advances is one readily recognized by those medical professionals who testify in any given case that, *even with early detection and adequate treatment*, the *patient-plaintiff's* chances fell below 50%.

Lastly, *as mentioned previously*, Weigand's contention arguably fails to recognize the sheer fact that there are those matters wherein which *early detection* would produce, *at the very least*, a chance for better results. While Weigand's arguments may implicitly recognize this reality, they *no less* fail to afford it any weight. *Ignoring the fact that Weigand solely focuses on cancer*, this speaks to a larger issue inherent in those scholarly publications and judicial decisions who view such posited concerns from the *crow's nest, rather than the deck*. While this will be addressed later on this text, *for now*, I will suggest that there is more to loss of chance than simply the survival aspect of proper diagnosis. Take for instance, *Lori Gordon*, who was led to believe she was suffering from anxiety and that her symptoms were all just some complex physical manifestation of her internal brain chemistry, when in reality, Lori's fears and symptoms were very real.[198]

While one may argue early diagnosis would have afforded Lori little to no recovery nor avoidance of the ultimate outcome, one could not deny that early diagnosis would have likely saved her from the assumed severe stress of believing it was "all in her head," the stress of feeling there is something wrong, *yet no one will listen, etc.*[199] Necessarily, one may argue that a *patient-plaintiff* in Lori's position is robbed of the ability to set their affairs in order, be there for their

---

[197] *See e.g.*, 836 N.W.2d 321; 126 N.M. 807; 255 Kan. 199; 481 Pa. 256; 146 Haw. 540; 828 S.W.2d 681; 393 N.W.2d 131; 691 A.2d 641; 734 N.E.2d 535; 2003 WY 91, *on reh'g* 2004 WY 44; 107 Nev. 1 (1991); 361 Or. 456; 1987 OK 69; 141 Ariz. 597; 498 So. 2d 713; 452 Mass. 1; 454 Mich. 639; 48 F.Supp.2d 924; and 272 S.W.3d 146.
[198] *Kemper v. Gordon*, 272 S.W.3d 146, 148-49 (Ky. 2008).
[199] *Gordon v. Kemper*, No. 2002-CA-001983-MR, Cross-Appeal No. 2002-CA-002043-MR, (Ky. Ct. App. Mar. 25, 2005) ("Lori believed that something was physically wrong with her. Lori was so fatigued that she could barely get out of bed and so nauseated that she could hardly eat. She reported hair loss, chronic urinary tract infections, and severe chest pains.").

family and children, and potentially ease or end their suffering *via* a number of means. This factual premise stands true, even if such *patient-plaintiff* would have still died with early detection and proper treatment. *Chance means something.*

DEFENSIVE MEDICINE

Lastly, another argument that has been advanced, contends that loss of chance recovery ought to be avoided, as it encourages defensive medicine.[200]

> Defensive medicine is defined as those tests, procedures, referrals, hospitalizations, or prescriptions ordered by physicians out of fear of being sued.[201]

In line with such practice, Tory Weigand has argued that "[n]o profession should feel it needs to diverge from the applicable standard of care or alter reasonable judgment and practice for fear of being sued."[202] While one could reasonably agree, *as I do*, with Weigand's statement, such correlation between *the loss of chance doctrine* and defensive medicine, has yet to be substantiated, as is the case with an increase in insurance premiums.[203] *In fact*, in support of Weigand's assertion he offers the following studies:

> In a recent study by the Massachusetts Medical Society, 83 percent of physicians polled reported practicing defensive medicine and that an average of 18 to 28 percent of tests, procedures, referrals, and consultations and 13 percent of hospitalizations were ordered for defensive reasons. The Massachusetts study estimated the cost of such practices conservatively at $1.4 million while another 2000 study

---

[200] Tory Weigand, Lost Chances, Felt Necessities, and the Tale of Two Cities, 43 Suffolk U. L. Rev. 327, 373 (2010) ("Additionally, imposing liability upon physicians for any statistical loss of a better outcome can only fuel defensive medicine.").

[201] *Id.* at 342–43 (2010).

[202] *Id.* at 343.

[203] Koch, *supra* note 167, at 626-30 ("various factors other than medical malpractice claims themselves appear to be the driving force behind the malpractice insurance premium rates... a particular state's adoption of the lost-chance doctrine is even more tangentially related to any potential effect that medical malpractice claims may have on malpractice insurance rates. . . .").

estimated the cost at $70 billion. Another related study found that an average of 44 to 48 percent of the physicians in Massachusetts reported that they alter or limit their practices because of the fear of being sued. Similarly, an earlier nation-wide study by the American Medical Association revealed that "seventy-nine percent of physicians reported that the 'fear of being sued' caused them to order more tests because of concerns of potential medical liability lawsuits." The result of defensive medicine is an increase in health care costs and ineffective and counterproductive medical care.[204]

Noticeably, all of these studies Weigand cited concern data that was collected in Massachusetts _prior_ to that State's adoption of the loss of chance doctrine in _Matsuyama_. Consequently, the results of these studies would seem to be of little use when it comes to arguing that the loss of chance doctrine has increased defensive medicine.

Looking ahead—appreciably, if one can truly value this doctrine's utility in its application in modern tort (_at least as it is confined to those actions concerning medical malpractice_) the unequivocal query now becomes, how might it be applied so as to _quell_ any of the concerns and quandaries advanced by _scholars_ and _courts_ around the Globe. _Equally important_, how can an approach to loss of chance be crafted so as to not only be _fair_ and _just_, but also be perceived as **fair** and **just** to those physicians who may be held culpable under it. To answer this question, the concept of "Physician Dissonance" is explored in the proceeding section, before presenting my own approach, _the Walker Approach_, to valuing loss of chance damages.

---

[204] Tory A. Weigand, _Lost Chances, Felt Necessities, and the Tale of Two Cities_, 43 Suffolk U. L. Rev. 327, 342–43 (2010).

Chapter 12

YOU'RE GONNA NEED A BIGGER BOAT

Preface — in this Chapter we explore the importance of utilizing an approach to loss of chance that is not only accepted by *patient-plaintiffs*, but also physicians and medical professionals alike. Ultimately, the conclusion is reached that any approach to loss of chance offered, arguably ought not only account for "Physician Dissonance," but in turn *seek to rectify it*.

Primer — *often times*, I have been known to present an argument through the vehicle of analogy to film. *Ergo*, when it comes to making the argument that I plan to advance in the proceeding pages, there is only one film that tends to do the trick. *What film you ask?* One that has been terrifying beachgoers since the summer of 1975. You guessed it, Jaws! For those who have never seen this masterpiece of a film, allow me to set the stage:

> The community of Amity, a small fictional island off the coast of New England, is stocked by a rogue Great White shark (not "*onjumanus* or *Isurus glaucus*," but rather, *Carcharodon carcharias*), resulting in a series of horrific attacks that threaten the business of this small seaside tourist-dependent town. When the first attack occurs, the *mainland loving* Chief Brody, seeks to close the beaches. However, such action is nullified almost immediately by Mayor Larry Vaughan, who

contends that the gruesome death resulted from a boat propeller accident, asserting there has never been a shark attack in Amity waters. In fact, Mayor Vaughan painstakingly maintains such denial throughout the film up until, for lack of a better phrase, "the shark is finally out of the bag." At which point, it's up to the *ironically aquaphobic* Chief Brody and his team, comprised of a green oceanographer and a seasoned Shark Hunter with a penchant for Narragansett Beer and piano wire, to get their Shark to *bite the ~~dust~~ bullet.*

If you have seen the film, then like many, you may be wondering why Chief Brody was able to recognize and acknowledge the presence of the Shark, while Mayor Vaughan, like many of the other individuals who sent their children into the waters following the attacks, maintained his position of denial. Interestingly, when discussing negligence, I have observed this same kind of denial or *nullification via rationalization* in my conversations with health care professionals. Appreciably, I explore the potential reasons for this stark dichotomy in viewpoint in the immediate section that follows.

PHYSICIAN DISSONANCE

Throughout my life I have managed to build relationships with medical professionals, many of whom are prominent and well-respected physicians, while others…not so much. This reality has enabled me to appreciate how those physicians, whom I have grown close to, view the law, and more importantly, the law surrounding medical negligence. It is through these relationships, that I have come to add an extra dimension to this text, affording me yet another reason to assert that the Walker Approach, which I advance in the next chapter, affords a more palatable solution to appreciating damages. That reason concerns the amelioration of cognitive dissonance.

The Phenomenon — I subscribe to the school of thought that if you want to market something successfully, *then necessarily*, you must know your audience. *As a grandson, nephew, and son*, I grew up surrounded and immersed within the health care industry, my early days spent sitting in on surgeries, talking to patients, *and when no one was looking*, playing with the high-speed torque surgical drill. From there, I went on to undertake health science studies and psychology, and later, *as a law student*, electing to collaborate with medical students to connect marginalized individuals to needed resources in the community.

Subsequently, in 2020, I created the Walker Health Law Moot, a *medical-legal* competition that gives law students the opportunity to strengthen their advocacy skills and display their talents in front of over 100 prominent legal and medical professionals. Appreciably, a fundamental goal of the event is to afford law students marketplace exposure (*thereby aiding in obtaining employment*), while dually enabling each the opportunity to engage more intimately with complex medical negligence cases. While this competition has been amazingly successful, garnering sponsorships from top-tier law firms, brands, organizations, and corporations, *such as Red Bull, McDonald's, Michigan State University, the Canadian Bar Association, Mothers Against Drunk Driving, LexisNexis, and Thomson Reuters*, **one of the chief joys has been building relationships with prominent physicians.**

All this to say, I have had sufficient time to interact with enough physicians and medical practitioners to know of their general feeling toward the word "negligence." That feeling, may very well be personified or captured in the beloved and somewhat overly used GIF of Homer Simpson slowly retreating into a hedge. This aversiveness to the word "negligence" often stemmed, *or reared itself*, from our discussions of cases whereupon, following a lengthy discourse concerning the factual *minutiae* of the case, the ultimate question presented itself, "*So, what do you think, was the physician negligent?*"

Despite the reality that the judges presiding over the actual case answered this question in the affirmative, 9/10 times the physician that I posed this question to would answer in the *negative*. One physician, a *well-respected* and *well-practiced* gastroenterologist, simply told me "Matt, one thing you've got to understand is, Sh** Happens." Another doctor, *who had been retired for years*, responded by stating the following to me: "If you hold every doctor liable for every single tiny mistake, as might as well get rid of medical schools, because who is going to want to be a doctor with that kind of pressure over their head." I want you to remember that word "**mistake**," as I will ask you to recall it later.

Apropos, why was there such a difference of opinion between those of the judiciary, and those physicians I questioned. After all, shouldn't the two opinions be aligned. Of course, opinions will differ between individuals, and results will vary by sample size (*comparably small sample size in this case, concerning those questioned*), but I noticed this difference arising enough to the point where I felt encouraged to explore the reasons for its occurrence.

The Feeling — naturally, like any *multi-faceted* scholar, I sought to delve deep within the tool chest that contains my various academic and life experiences to see whether I could potentially postulate some satisfactory theorem. Accordingly, *via* chain of reasoning, *cognitive dissonance* afforded such solution.

In 2017, I undertook the challenge of trying to educate and prevent individuals from operating vehicles while under the influence of marijuana. To do so, I utilized a social media platform and, among other methods of education, actively began challenging individuals who had for instance, bragged about "driving high," getting in a vehicle with a "high driver," etc. While the project began as an applied social psychology experiment, it quickly took on a life of its own thereafter. My goal, was to bring about attitudinal change by taking advantage of this psychological theory referred to as cognitive dissonance.

After all, like any other member of society, physicians themselves are not immune from cognitive dissonance, a social psychology theory that has been deemed one of the most influential to have arisen from within that field.[205] Appreciably, I believe that this reality speaks to the commonality I have observed amongst those physicians I have spoken with, whom when confronted with a physician's negligence, seek to explain it away, or relate their aversion to the judiciary's decision. Now, for those who missed out on applied social psychology, or just happened to fall asleep during the cognitive dissonance lectures, allow me to elaborate on this psychological wonderment.

As one who is well versed in *metaphysics*, perhaps, *at least in my opinion*, cognitive dissonance is best described as the psychological phenomenon taking hold within the construct portrayed in Plato's *Allegory of the Cave.* In Plato's *Allegory of the Cave, Plato* records the dialogue between his sibling, *Glaucon*, and *Socrates*, in which *Socrates's* orally depicts a group of prisoners bound by chain to one another and confined within an underground cavern for all of their lives.[206] Behind them, exists a massive fire, and between them and this fire stands a partition through which shadows are cast by puppeteers.[207] *Paralyzed by shackles*, all they can do is look at the cave wall upon which these shadows dance.[208]

Necessarily, since the prisoners cannot see the puppeteers behind them, they believe the figures and objects cast are real.[209] In fact, since this reality is all they have known from the time of infancy,

---

[205] Eddie Harmon-Jones & Judson Mills, *An Introduction to Cognitive Dissonance Theory and an Overview of Current Perspectives on the Theory, in Cognitive dissonance: Reexamining a pivotal theory in psychology* (2nd ed.) 3–24, at 3 (Eddie Harmon-Jones ed., 2019), http://content.apa.org/books/16109-001.

[206] Shawn Eyer, *Translation from Plato's Republic 514b–518d* ("*Allegory of the Cave*"), Harvard Uni. Pub. (2009), https://scholar.harvard.edu/files/seyer/files/plato_republic_514b-518d_allegory-of-the-cave.pdf; and *see also Plato's Allegory of the Cave Explained*, MasterClass (Nov. 2021 Update), https://www.masterclass.com/articles/allegory-of-the-cave-explained.

[207] *Id.*

[208] *Id.*

[209] *Id.*

understandably, it is believed to be the <u>only</u> reality.[210] With their heads facing directly forward, *what they see, is all that exists.*[211] At least, such is the case until one prisoner is set loose, free of those confining chains, and made to look behind him:

PLATO'S ALLEGORY OF THE CAVE

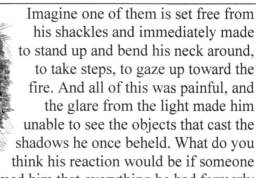

Imagine one of them is set free from his shackles and immediately made to stand up and bend his neck around, to take steps, to gaze up toward the fire. And all of this was painful, and the glare from the light made him unable to see the objects that cast the shadows he once beheld. What do you think his reaction would be if someone informed him that everything he had formerly known was illusion and delusion, but that now he was a few steps closer to reality, oriented now toward things that were more authentic, and able to see more truly? And, even further, if one would direct his attention to the artificial figures passing to and fro and ask him what their names are, would this man not be at a loss to do so? Would he, rather, believe that the shadows he formerly knew were more real than the objects now being shown to him? Glaukon: Much more real. Socrates: Now, if he was forced to look directly at the firelight, wouldn't his eyes be pained? Wouldn't he turn away and run back to those things which he normally perceived and understand them as more defined and clearer than the things now being brought to his attention? Glaukon: That's right.[212]

I put to you, why would this *once* prisoner seek to turn away, grab hold of normality, and ignore this newly presented reality? *It's because of "That Feeling."*

---

[210] *Id.*
[211] *Id.*
[212] *Id.*

AIR DISSONANCE

Cognitive dissonance refers to that feeling we get when we are confronted with information and thoughts that go against the beliefs, perceptions, feelings, and attitudes we hold...

It is that feeling you get when you pick up a carton of ice cream and read the ingredients before putting spoon to mouth; it is that uncomfortableness that creeps into your consciousness when someone tells you that you did not get the job you wanted; and it is that hesitation that takes hold for *sheer moments* when you purchase another pair of Nike Air Jordans, knowing very well that you just ordered two pairs the week before.

Okay, maybe that last one only applies to me, *but the point still stands*. You see we interact *with* and *encounter* cognitive dissonance every single day. It is a mechanism of cognition, the very essence of which we both control and are controlled by. *As puppeteer stands to puppet*, the methods we employ to reduce such dissonance, can operate at such a deeply entrenched level that we often have little awareness of it.

In other words, cognitive dissonance theory suggests that when an individual is confronted with *dissonant cognitions*, they experience psychological discomfort, which motivates them to decrease such dissonance.[213] How might one go about reducing this dissonance? Amongst other strategies, simply by avoiding such inflammatory information.[214]

---

[213] Eddie Harmon-Jones & Judson Mills, *An Introduction to Cognitive Dissonance Theory and an Overview of Current Perspectives on the Theory*, in Cognitive dissonance: Reexamining a pivotal theory in psychology (2nd ed.) 3–24 (Eddie Harmon-Jones ed., 2019), http://content.apa.org/books/16109-001.
[214] *Id.*

Take for instance the following scenario utilized and offered by Leon Festinger in 1957:

> A habitual smoker who learns that smoking is bad for health will experience dissonance because the knowledge that smoking is bad for health is dissonant with the cognition that he continues to smoke. He can reduce the dissonance by changing his behavior, that is, he could stop smoking, which would be consonant with the cognition that smoking is bad for health. Alternatively, the smoker could reduce dissonance by changing his cognition about the effect of smoking on health and believe that smoking does not have a harmful effect on health (eliminating the dissonant cognition). He might look for positive effects of smoking and believe that smoking reduces tension and keeps him from gaining weight (adding consonant cognitions). Or he might believe that the risk to health from smoking is negligible compared with the danger of automobile accidents (reducing the importance of the dissonant cognition). In addition, he might consider the enjoyment he gets from smoking to be a very important part of his life (increasing the importance of consonant cognitions).[215]

Ineludibly, such elimination or reduction of dissonance was likely what I was witnessing in each interaction, wherein which I posed to each medical professional the negligence *query* previously detailed herein. While such nullification of culpability can be due to a number of factors, such as fear of speaking out against a colleague, collegiality, membership and group-identity, or possibly the *unwritten "do not testify rule*," it is my belief that cognitive dissonance plays a prominent role.[216]

---

[215] *Id.* at 4.

[216] *See* Michael Flynn, *The Unwritten Rules of Sports and Medical Malpractice*, 19 J. Health Care L. & Pol'y 73, 77 (2017):

> The "conspiracy of silence" among doctors embodies the notion that testifying against a fellow doctor in a medical malpractice case is akin to betrayal and is grounds for punishment. This "conspiracy of silence" has led to an implicit reluctance from members of the medical community to testify on behalf of plaintiffs and has established an unwritten rule among medical professionals of not testifying against your fellow doctor. Anyone who breaks this rule is dubbed a traitor and publicly labeled a "hired gun," embodying the idea that expert witnesses are for

I say this, having dedicated myself for five years to the study of psychology and being presented with a medal for my academic achievement within the Faculty of Science by my undergraduate institution. But, to further cement this witnessed sentiment (*i.e., dissonance with negligence*) allow me to provide both a factual extract and the testimony of my former physician, Dr. Hagen, who served as an expert for the defendant, Dr. Ward, in the precedential case of *Armstrong v. Royal Victoria Hospital, 2019 ONCA 963*.

ARMSTRONG V. WARD

In *Armstrong*, the patient brought suit against Dr. Ward, asserting that he negligently utilized a LigaSure (*cauterizing device*), resulting in tissue scarring or adhesions that considerably blocked the patient's left ureter and led to kidney damage, the surgical removal of which became necessary thereafter.[217] Notably, the Supreme Court of Canada ultimately found Dr. Ward negligent, *but of practical importance here*, was the testimony utilized on appeal just prior to this final ruling. Appreciably, Dr. Hagen was touted as an expert in causation and the requisite standard of care, and he estimated himself to have used the LigaSure (*i.e., the cauterizing device that harmed the patient*) thousands of times, with no such injury to a patient's ureter ever occurring.[218] Necessarily, in an effort to enable one the ability to fully appreciate the point I will soon make, I have gone to the trouble of reproducing Dr. Hagen's testimony over the proceeding pages.

---

sale and that attorneys can actively shop for those willing to support their cause. In fact, the problem has become so widespread that the "so-called conspiracy of silence has been recognized as a matter of judicial notice [across the country]."
[217] *Armstrong v. Royal Victoria Hospital*, 2019 ONCA 963; and *Armstrong v. Ward*, 2021 SCC 1.
[218] 2019 ONCA 963, at para. 106.

DR. HAGEN'S TESTIMONY

Q. Now, Dr. Hagen, I want you to assume that Dr. Ward, at the time of the laparoscopic colectomy, mobilized the left colon using a combination of cautery and blunt dissection and using the medial approach, Dr. Ward moved the colon upward toward the anterior abdominal wall, something he calls tenting. He then proceeded to identify the ureter visually through the laparoscope and either touched or pushed structures around the ureter to observe it move or vermiculate. Once the ureter is identified visually, using blunt dissection, he moved the retroperitoneal structures, where the ureter is located, away from the colon. Now stopping there, do those steps, are those steps reasonable in the identification and protection of the left ureter?

A. Yes.

Q. And do those steps meet the standard of care in the identification and protection of the left ureter from injury during a laparosopic colectomy?

A. Yes.

Q. I then want you to assume that once the ureter has been identified and pushed away, that Dr. Ward opened the LigaSure package and divided the colonic mesentery with the LigaSure going on the diagram you have there, Exhibit 2, from right to left, circumferentially, staying away from the ureter and near the colon. And Dr. Hagen, does that step I've asked you to assume, to divide the colonic mesentery with the LigaSure, is that a reasonable way of doing it?

A. Yes.

Q. And does that way of dividing the colonic mesentery meet the standard of care?

A. Yes

(...)

Q. I want to talk about the standard of care. You will agree with me, I think, that the standard of care for benign colon surgery is to identify the ureter and then stay away from the area.

A. That's correct.

Q. And you have to stay far enough away from the ureter that your instruments don't inadvertently injure.

A. Yes.

Q. Now you testified that you have, in your own practice, not seen a case in which a ureter has been injured using a LigaSure device, correct?

A. Actually, that's not totally – I have seen LigaSure injury of the ureter, yes.

Q. Okay, in your own practice?

A. No, like but I have, I have seen it in video and you know, discussing with colleagues and things like that. But I have a teaching video of that.

Q. I wish we had that. You haven't had any cases, yourself, in which your patients have been injured with a LigaSure on the ureter.

A. Not to my knowledge, no.

Q. And the reason for that is because when you are using the LigaSure device, you stay as far away from the ureter as possible.

A. That's correct.

Q. And certainly, you stay more than two millimetres away from the ureter.

A. Yes.

Q. Always.

A. Well, I would...to answer your question I would try and stay away from the ureter, you know, more than two millimetres.

Q. Right, and the reason you would do that is because you don't want to inadvertently damage the ureter with the LigaSure.

A. Yes.

(...)

Q. ...you'll agree with me if ...Dr. Ward used the LigaSure device within two millimetres of the ureter either because he made a mistake with the LigaSure, he misidentified the anatomy, he got lost, whatever, if he did that, that was a breach of the standard of care?

A. I wouldn't agree with that, no.

Q. Okay, so your opinion today is that it would not be a breach of the standard of care to operate the LigaSure device within two millimetres of the ureter.

A. I would, I would qualify that in the sense that if you, you have to identify the ureter and take precautions to not, you know, to know where it is and, if you did that, it would not be a breach of the standard of care.

Q. So let's uncap this...what you're saying, I think, is if you have done that, if you have properly identified and protected the ureter, then you wouldn't have this injury.

A. Yes.

Q. And the reason you wouldn't have this injury is because you wouldn't put the LigaSure two millimetres away from the ureter.

A. Yes.

Q. Right, once you, once you know where the ureter is, you're going to stay away from it.

A. That's correct.

Q. That's what you're saying.

A. Yeah.

Q. Now what I'm asking you to assume because the court is ultimately going to have to decide what happened here.

A. Right.

Q. We don't have a time machine, we can't go back and look, I want you to assume that Dr. Klotz and Dr. Burnstein are correct and that for whatever reason, Dr. Ward used the LigaSure within two millimetres. It has to be an accident. Nobody is suggesting that he did it intentionally.

A. Right.

Q. But that he did that. And now what I'm suggesting to you is that if you assume that that is correct, that Dr. Ward breached the standard of care.

A. No, I don't agree with that.

Q. So if Dr. Ward is mistaken in his identification and protection of the ureter and as a result of that mistake, uses the LigaSure within two millimetres of the ureter, thereby causing damage to the ureter, your opinion is that would meet the standard of care, is that what you're saying?

A. Yes.

Q. All right. Well, what would be the point in trying to identify and protect the ureter? That's actually a question.

A. What's the point? The point of identifying the ureter is to avoid injuring it.

Q. And if you're using the LigaSure, which we know has a thermal spread of two millimetres – you've agreed with that already.

A. I agree with that, yes.

Q. And the point of identifying it is so that you can stay more than two millimetres away, isn't that right?

A. Yes.

Q. And this is a, we're talking about a general principle that applies to surgery in general, right? Anybody who is doing surgery in this area has to know about the ureter and has to take steps to protect it.

A. Right.

> Q. Right. It doesn't matter whether you're a general surgeon or a urologist or an obstetrician or some other surgeon in the area, you agree with that.
>
> A. Yes.
>
> Q. And it doesn't matter whether you're doing it open or laparoscopically.
>
> A. Yes.[219]

Now, you may be asking yourself what exactly was the "big deal" with Dr. Hagen's testimony, *or better yet*, what exactly stands out from the above extract? Simply put, *at the microscopic level*, what you may be observing is how Dr. Hagen seems to outright contradict himself, *while at the broader level*, you may gain a better sense of what I call "Physician Dissonance."

Dealing with the former first, Dr. Hagen testifies *quite clearly* that the standard of care for benign colon surgery is, *quite plainly*, to locate the patient's ureter and thereafter stay at least two-millimeters away from that area.[220] Importantly, Dr. Hagen asserts that if the physician follows this crucial step, then the injury, *which ultimately occurred*, would not have been possible.[221] Despite this however, Dr. Hagen goes on to testify that if Dr. Ward came within two millimeters of the ureter, he would not have breached the standard of care.[222]

Upon reading this testimony, I am recalled to that well-known scene from the Pink Panther, in which the infamous inspector Jacques Clouseau, with the help of a dialect coach, attempts to master the sentence, "*I would like to buy a hamburger*." After disastrously, and quite humorously, failing to say the sentence, Clouseau's dialect coach endeavors to arrive at a solution by having Clouseau break

---

[219] 2019 ONCA 963, at paras. 107-10.

[220] 2019 ONCA 963, at paras. 107-10.

[221] 2019 ONCA 963, at paras. 109.

[222] 2019 ONCA 963, at paras. 109 ("Dr. Hagen confirmed that it was necessary for the surgeon to stay two millimetres away from the ureter and that if the surgeon had properly identified and protected the ureter "you wouldn't have this injury". However he refused to admit that Dr. Ward might have failed to do so, or if he did that he would have breached the standard of care…").

down the sentence *somewhat* phonetically. Surprisingly, Clouseau manages to master each individual word, but when asked to put them together (*i.e., form a string of words*), he once again, hilariously fails.

In our excerpt above, plaintiff's counsel, *like Clouseau's dialect coach*, attempts to get Dr. Hagen to break down the standard of care *piece by piece*. However, the moment he is asked to put everything together (*i.e., the moment Dr. Ward's name is applied to the scenario*), Dr. Hagen seems unable to, *or perhaps is simply unwilling to*, connect the dots. This latter point brings me to the phenomenon I have termed "Physician Dissonance." Here, it can be argued that in breaking down the standard of care and speaking in generalities and abstractions, counsel for the plaintiff was promulgating a line of questioning with attributes evocative of first-order logic. In other words, Dr. Hagen was faced with a line of questioning that amounted to "For all x, if x uses the LigaSure within two millimeters of the ureter, then x is negligent." For those unfamiliar with first-order logic, allow me to translate:

> The idea is simply that if counsel can get Dr. Hagen to accept the premise that if a *physician* uses the LigaSure within two millimeters of the ureter, then *that physician* is negligent, counsel should similarly have no problem when *physician* (x) is replaced with *Dr. Ward* (x). While the subject changes, the predicates remain, as does the truth Dr. Hagen initially assigned to the statement. Despite this, *and against logic*, Dr. Hagen manages to change his position once Dr. Ward's name is inserted. Why is that?

Of course, this is just my opinion, and Dr. Hagen could have responded as he did **for a variety of reasons**. However, *I believe* it may come down to the dissonance Dr. Hagan could have experienced the moment that the subject changed from *physician in the abstract*, to *Dr. Ward*. To see why this conclusion is logical, one must appreciate the position Dr. Hagen was in, having been brought on by the defendant to serve as his expert, *his champion*. I am not suggesting in any way that Dr. Hagen proffered any intentional misrepresentation or engaged in dishonesty. However, I am offering up the opinion that Dr. Hagen's conflicting testimony stems potentially from the fact that he was presented with information that contradicted his *raison d'être* as testifier in this matter. <u>Again, this is just my **opinion** as an outside observer (*reader*), and in no way is it meant to be construed as asserting a statement of fact.</u>

To illustrate this effect further, allow me to offer up yet another example in which it can be observed. Apologies in advance for this example, but it truly helps bring home the point:

> From approximately 1974, and thereafter spanning a period of 15 years, Ted Bundy carried out a series of killings, taking the lives of approximately 30 victims. While Bundy was eventually convicted and executed, his mother unceasingly professed her child's innocence. Following, her son's conviction, Bundy's mother stated, "Ted Bundy does not go around killing women and little children! ... Our never-ending faith in Ted – our faith that he is innocent – has never wavered. And it never will." Such a fact remained true, even after her son confessed and provided details of the crimes he committed.[223]

Why is it that Louise Bundy could not see her son as a serial killer? What was the reason for her denial? If one subscribes to the theory of cognitive dissonance, perhaps it is reasonable to say Ms. Bundy was faced with conflicting information: *on one hand*, Ted was her son, the boy she raised and loved, who "grew up in none other than a good, solid, Christian home with two parents";[224] *on the other hand*, she is not only being told by the media and the court, but through the mouth of her own son, that he committed these horrific crimes.

---

[223] Katie Serena, *Meet Ted Bundy's Mom, Eleanor Louise Cowell, Who Never Questioned His Innocence*, ati (2019), https://allthatsinteresting.com/eleanor-louise-cowell.
[224] *Id.*

Perhaps, it then becomes reasonable to assume that should Ms. Bundy accept as true this new information she is being presented with, she must then also except that she was a *terrible mother*, or that she raised a serial killer.[225]

For many parents, accepting either of those latter premises would pose a bitter pill to swallow, *and yet*, many would, whilst others would remain stagnant in *denial*. This is the foothold through which cognitive dissonance is best exemplified.[226] In my opinion, it is one of the main reasons why many of the physicians I speak with, read about, or observe in my Moot competition, are unwilling to recognize negligence in their peers, or instead, see negligence and malpractice as *unfair (or plaintiff-friendly)*.

In fact, upon posing the question presented at the beginning of this chapter, one health care professional confessed to me, "if I say that this physician is negligent, then where does the line get drawn. You can't hold every physician liable for making a simple mistake."

---

[225] Eddie Harmon-Jones & Judson Mills, *An Introduction to Cognitive Dissonance Theory and an Overview of Current Perspectives on the Theory, in Cognitive dissonance: Reexamining a pivotal theory in psychology* (2nd ed.) 3–24, at 4 (Eddie Harmon-Jones ed., 2019), http://content.apa.org/books/16109-001.

[226] Yet another example of cognitive dissonance can be found in the following fictional scenario: Chris, a 12-year-old with a proclivity for luxury items and fast-food, has a parent, Mrs. Kroc, who believes her child can do no wrong. In fact, over the years, Mrs. Kroc has spoiled Chris to no end, resulting in him being ill-disciplined, entitled, and egocentrically-regressed. Well, Chris ended up getting into a fist-fight with *Randy*, another student at school, and was subsequently brought to the principal's office. Despite this, no punishment ever was handed down to Chris. Instead, blame fell upon Randy, an individual who was dwarfed in size by Chris. Why you ask? Chris showed his mother text messages from Randy that suggested Randy was bullying Chris, and in fact, was the one who initiated the fight. Armed with this information, Mrs. Kroc had the principal suspend Randy and issue a formal apology to Chris. The one problem is, the text messages Chris showed to his mother were completely fabricated by Chris and his friend Bob. When Randy finds out, he tells Mrs. Kroc and the Principal, and even goes so far as to show them both how the text messages were faked, but Mrs. Kroc refuses to believe that her son would do such a thing, after all, she exclaims, "Chris is the most honest boy in the world." Why do you think Mrs. Kroc would refuse to believe, or even question her son, in the face of such new information?

It is at this point we arrive at the crux of my argument, and you will recall that I asked you to keep in mind the word "mistake." Physicians, *if I can generalize*, likely do not appreciate being held liable for what they deem "mere mistakes." Certainly, it may be argued that were one to introduce the "chance" for physicians to be held liable for the chances they deny their patients, this would create even further dissonance, *that in turn*, may result in defensive measures being undertaken.[227] Perhaps Tory Weigand said it best, when he stated the following argument:

> "Moreover, if statistical chances, no matter how small, are the basis for liability, why wouldn't healthcare providers simply order any and all testing and procedure regardless of efficacy?"[228]

While this statement undoubtedly speaks to the defensive medicine argument highlighted earlier in this text, it also speaks implicitly to "Physician Dissonance."

So, how might one go about removing such fears as Weigand's, *with respect to defensive medicine*, or those of physicians who may fear being held liable for "mistakes" when it comes to loss of chance. First, one might emphasize, as I have done in my discourse on this topic with medical professionals, that the statistical chances that are the basis for liability only receive "teeth" because a physician is deemed by his peers to have failed to meet the standard of care.[229]

---

[227] Tory A. Weigand, *Lost Chances, Felt Necessities, and the Tale of Two Cities*, 43 Suffolk U. L. Rev. 327, 373 (2010) ("[a]dditionally, imposing liability upon physicians for any statistical loss of a better outcome can only fuel defensive medicine.").
[228] *Id.* at 373.
[229] 272 S.W.3d at 161 ("Lost chance is never reached by the trier of fact unless it also finds that a physician acted negligently toward his or her patient.").

Secondly, *and this point cannot be stressed enough*, to suggest that any *patient-plaintiff* could recover for the lost chance, "no matter how small," fails to appreciate that most *patient-plaintiffs* would likely be deterred from what little recovery they would receive (*i.e., small loss of chance → small damages*) in the face of *burdensome* court costs.[230]

Thirdly, to advance the case that healthcare providers should be afraid that they will be held negligent for loss of chance if they do not order every single test, largely *misconstrues* the very notion of negligence.[231] In doing so, one confusingly conflates "simple mistakes" (*that do not violate the standard of care*) with those rising to the level of negligence. This follows, as if a battery of tests is deemed within the standard care by expert witnesses at trial, then necessarily those tests must be performed.

Apropos, it would be folly to suggest that healthcare providers would be held to have breached the standard of care in failing to "order any and all testing and procedure regardless of efficacy."[232] *A fortiori*, testing that serves no value, nor boasts any efficacy, would logically not fall within the standard of care, unless it was efficacious and of value.

---

[230] Tory A. Weigand, *Lost Chances, Felt Necessities, and the Tale of Two Cities*, 43 Suffolk U. L. Rev. 327, 373 (2010); and 272 S.W.3d at 152 ("Yet, under this doctrine, even a small percentage of the value of a human life could generate substantial recovery and place burdensome costs on healthcare providers.").

[231] Tory A. Weigand, *Lost Chances, Felt Necessities, and the Tale of Two Cities*, 43 Suffolk U. L. Rev. 327, 373 (2010) ("Moreover, if statistical chances, no matter how small, are the basis for liability, why wouldn't healthcare providers simply order any and all testing and procedure regardless of efficacy?").

[232] *Id.* at 373.

Arguably, Weigand's assertion, like many of the concerns this text has explored, seems to appeal more to *fear*, never presenting any "real" correlation with rising insurance, fear, or increases in malpractice claims with adoption of this doctrine. It is simply *fear-mongering*. Ultimately, if one were to champion an approach to loss of chance valuation, one would need to ensure that such approach advances a methodology for recovery logically linking damages to actual harm. In doing so, the aim would be to enable (1) physicians to recognize that liability for loss of chance solely stems from conduct that is negligent; and (2) if recovery is afforded, such compensation will *proportionally* reflect the actual harm the physician is responsible for.

Appreciably, such an approach could reasonably reduce "Physician Dissonance" in facilitating alteration of cognitions concerning not only the law of negligence (*more specifically, medical malpractice*), *but more importantly*, the application of loss of chance and the notion that liability *shall* fall on only those who are negligent (*removing dissonant cognitions concerning non-negligent mistakes*).

A look ahead —the point of this chapter was to explore cognitive dissonance in an effort to account for another potential factor for which any proposed approach to loss of chance ought to consider. *Having now discussed this topic*, we move on to consider *the Walker Approach*.

Chapter 13

THE WALKER APPROACH
BRINGING BALANCE TO THE TORT

The below account reflects "the profoundly sad" details of the events leading to the disturbing death of Lori Gordon, a young mother, for whom the Supreme Court of Kentucky denied application of the loss of chance doctrine.[233] *Kemper v. Gordon*, 272 S.W.3d 146, 148–50 (Ky. 2008):

> In early February 1996, Lori, then thirty-eight years of age and otherwise in good health, suddenly experienced chest pain, shortness of breath, severe nausea, and dizziness. She was admitted to Baptist Hospital East for a cardiovascular evaluation which was conducted by Dr. George Stacy. When Lori's tests all appeared within normal limits, Dr. Stacy ruled out any cardiovascular cause and discharged Lori with directions to follow-up with her primary care physician if her symptoms reoccurred. On April 14th, while seeing a movie with one of her children, Lori again experienced chest pain and nausea. She was transported by ambulance to Baptist Hospital East and examined by Dr. Charles Smith in the emergency

---

[233] 272 S.W.3d at 147–52 ("We are troubled by the potential financial burden that might be spread upon the shoulders of millions of people if we adopt this new concept of lost or diminished chance of recovery.").

room. Finding no medical cause for Lori's symptoms, Dr. Smith prescribed Ativan for anxiety and recommended she see an internist. The next day, April 15th, Lori visited the office of Dr. Warren Kemper. Dr. Kemper ordered an ultrasound of her gallbladder. When the results of this test came back within normal limits, Dr. Kemper prescribed Xanax for anxiety. When Lori later phoned to inform him of her continued nausea, Dr. Kemper ordered a Computed Axial Tomography (CAT) scan of her abdomen. When the results of the CAT scan proved to be within normal limits, Dr. Kemper believed he had ruled out all possible physical causes for Lori's symptoms and reached the opinion that Lori suffered from anxiety and/or panic attacks. Dr. Kemper provided Lori with the names of several psychiatrists...Lori saw Dr. Lawrence Mudd, a psychiatrist, in June and July. Dr. Mudd also diagnosed Lori with anxiety disorder and began treating her with medications. In late August of 1996, as Lori's nausea and chest pain continued, she sought out the care of a new internist, Dr. Robert Ellis. Dr. Ellis, also unable to identify a medical explanation for Lori's symptoms, continued to treat her for anxiety. Lori then turned to psychologist, Dr. Carol Massey, in September, and a new psychiatrist, Dr. Karen Head, in October. In December, Lori came under the care of yet another psychiatrist, Dr. Kenneth Davis. Throughout this time, each of Lori's healthcare providers continued to treat her for anxiety and/or panic attacks. Lori's symptoms persisted, and on December 11, 1996, she was again taken to the emergency room at Baptist Hospital East complaining of chest pain. Lori was seen in the emergency room by Dr. Theodore Ivanchek. When a medical cause for her symptoms could not be determined, Lori was released. On December 21, 1996, Lori again went to the emergency room. On this occasion, she was examined by Dr. Jim Sharp. Once Dr. Sharp ruled out any possible cardiac causes, he released Lori with the recommendation that she follow-up with her primary care physician. Lori saw Dr. Ellis on December 27, 1996. In addition to her symptoms of nausea and chest pain, Lori described coughing up blood, discomfort in the region of her left chest, and weight loss (by this time she was down to 117 pounds). Once again, Lori underwent a cardiac evaluation by Dr. Stacy. In January of 1997, Dr. Ellis confirmed Lori had an enlarged lymph node and an unidentified mass on her neck. Dr. Ellis referred Lori to a surgeon, Dr. Chipman, who performed a biopsy. On February 3, 1997, Dr. Chipman informed Lori that both masses contained carcinoma, and the next day she was admitted to Alliant Hospital under the care of Dr. Don Stevens. A CAT scan of her abdomen and pelvis revealed extensive adenopathy. The diagnosis at that time was metastasized gastric (stomach) cancer. Sadly, on January 13, 1998, Lori died as a result of complications from gastric cancer. Prior to her death, she had filed claims against Dr. Kemper and others... The jury...eventually returned a verdict in favor of all three medical providers... If the jury had been allowed to find within a reasonable probability that had Lori's cancer been diagnosed on her first visit to Dr. Kemper her chance of recovery would have been 30%, but that at the actual time her cancer was finally discovered her chance of recovery had become only 5%, the Gordons would then have been entitled to recover 25% of the total damages resulting from Lori's death....[234]

Recall, in the context of medical negligence, a *patient-plaintiff* is afforded full recovery where, *at the time of the negligent diagnosis*, their initial chance was greater than 50%. However, for patients like Lori Gordon, with an initial chance that falls below this requisite threshold (*i.e., Lori's initial chance was 30%*), jurisdictions like Kentucky, Canada, the United Kingdom, and Australia, have denied such recovery for the chance lost.

Conversely, a majority of states in the U.S. have applied the loss of chance doctrine, widely valuing damages *via* the *proportional damages approach*.[235] Appreciably, while such application of this doctrine is arguably valuable, reliance on the *proportional damages approach* is sheer folly. This follows, as *unfair* and *nonsensical*

---

[234] 272 S.W.3d at 148–50.
[235] 452 Mass. at 26 ("The most widely adopted of these methods of valuation is the 'proportional damages' approach."); 836 N.W.2d at 335; and *Cahoon v. Cummings*, 734 N.E.2d 535, 541 (Ind. 2000).

outcomes result, with prototypical *physician-defendant* trapped in an empty room, walls closing in, forced to face the cold steel of the menacing "Spikes of Doom". *Superfluity of words aside*, in any such case, where the *patient-plaintiff's* initial chance of recovery or survival was above 50%, a negligent defendant will be liable to pay full damages; whereas, should such initial chance be deemed below 51%, only a proportionate amount is owed. *Necessarily*, this outcome has made jurisdictions wary of accepting the loss of chance doctrine:

> Part of what makes courts wary of the lost chance doctrine is the unnecessary complication created by assuming that lost chance only applies if there is a 50% chance or less that a better outcome was lost due to the failure to diagnose. This is the wrong approach. The cause of action cannot intelligently be divided by looking at causation on a continuum where the jury finds the negligence of the physician to be a substantial factor, 51% or better, in causing the patient's injury, but then tacking lost chance of a better recovery into that analysis by saying that anything 50% or less should be compensable because of the lost chance. This is mixing apples and oranges.[236]

However, yet another issue arises upon cogitating the formulaic mechanism through which calculation of damages is achieved. As stated previously, loss of chance has traditionally been computed *via* subtracting *post-negligence* chance of survival from *pre-negligence* chance of survival.[237] Ultimately, it is my belief that this method for calculating loss of chance damages is statistically flawed, as it fails to yield nothing more than a percentage point.

Accordingly, in an effort to rectify this "mistake" (*or fundamental oversight*) of Brobdingnagian proportions, I sought to develop my own approach for calculating loss of chance damages. Appreciably, in recommending my own approach, my motives are *threefold*:

---

[236] 272 S.W.3d at 159 (Noble, J., dissenting).
[237] 452 Mass. at 26; 836 N.W.2d at 335; and 734 N.E.2d at 541.

(1) I, *like many scholars*, truly believe that loss of chance is a real injury that necessarily ought to be compensable in the context of medical negligence;

(2) I believe that the loss of chance doctrine's *proportional damages approach* is axiomatically inapt at properly valuing chance; *and*

(3) I believe that the damages awarded in a medical negligence action ought to be dually meaningful and necessarily tied to the consequences of the wrongdoer's negligence, rather than center upon the fulfillment of, *what may only be deemed*, a statistically arbitrary threshold.

Put another way, this latter motive encapsulates my view that damages ought to be *proportionate* to the harm caused. Accordingly, to grasp how this result is effectively achieved, I present a detailed overview of my approach in the proceeding section.

BRASS TAX

Recall, loss of chance has traditionally been computed *via* subtracting *post-negligence* chance of survival from *pre-negligence* chance of survival.[238] Comparably, the *Walker Approach* provides a sound statistical analysis contrary to that which is offered by the *proportionate damages* calculation. This follows, as the issue with the *proportional damages approach* is twofold, with application of the loss of chance doctrine failing both *dimensionally* and *terminologically*.

Dimensionally speaking, accepting an approach that relies heavily on a continuum, *which defines the relevant threshold*, is greatly and detrimentally problematic. Consequently, if *the loss of chance doctrine* were introduced in Canada for instance, the courts would essentially be superimposing a *pro rata* recovery approach on

---

[238] 452 Mass. at 26; 836 N.W.2d at 335; and 734 N.E.2d at 541.

top of an *all or nothing* approach (*i.e.*, 50% threshold). Not surprisingly, *and as previously highlighted*, courts have grappled with this result, as it appears both counter-intuitive and unfair to hold a physician liable for full damages, *where chance is above 50%*, and for a proportion, *where chance falls below*.[239]

Ineluctably, the playing field — *i.e., the continuum* — on which analysis of the loss of chance is carried out, must be stripped away, with analysis grounded elsewhere. Necessarily, rectifying the issue of improper statistical terminology will lend credence to this argument, and will itself, provide a proper calculatory mechanism for correct analysis.

"SEVEN TIMES THIRTEEN EQUALS TWENTY-EIGHT

Ad absurdam, courts have widely statistically valued loss of chance by subtracting *post-negligence* survival chance from *pre-negligence* survival chance. This is quite problematic, as such subtraction only offers a percentage point, rather than an actual meaningful percentage of change. Unequivocally, it is well known amongst statisticians, when ascertaining solely the difference between two percentages, subtracting one value from the other is the requisite method for calculation. The value achieved through subtraction, characterizable as the percentage point, is absolute. Stated differently, the percentage point only offers a description of distance relative to nothing, whereas, a percent difference offers a relative value, *i.e., the percent difference relative to two percentages*, through which defining meaningful increase and decrease is made possible.[240]

Accordingly, when a patient's chance of survival or recovery has been diminished, it would be grossly incorrect to assess damages

---

[239] 272 S.W.3d at 159 (Noble, J., dissenting).

[240] *Percentage Change and Percentage Point Change: A Primer*, www.reed.edu (2010), https://www.reed.edu/percent (last visited Apr. 15, 2022); and Alvan R. Feinstein, *Invidious Comparisons and Unmet Clinical Challenges*, 92 AM. J. Med. 117 (1992).

using an absolute value. This follows, as that value truly means nothing in the context of a medical malpractice claim. Conversely, relying on a relative value to calculate damages, *in this context*, offers true statistical meaning, as it indicates actual loss. Significantly, percent difference indicates what percent, *i.e., the amount of chance*, was lost in relation to the value of *pre-negligence* and *post-negligence*, rather than a scale difference. Consequently, a method deemed statistically sound would seek to achieve the percent difference.

Accordingly, I modified the *proportional damages approach*, in an effort to craft the following mechanism for procuring a percent difference...

THE WALKER APPROACH

(1) What are the full damages to which the plaintiff would have been entitled had a causal link been established between the outcome and negligence?

The full amount to which the plaintiff would be entitled, had "but for" causation been satisfied.

(2) What was chance of survival or recovery pre-negligence?

Option at this point to argue, based on patient specific statistical analysis, patient falls above or below the distribution of survival.[241]

(3) What was the patient's chance of survival post-negligence?

(4) Subtract post-negligence survival from pre-negligence survival

= *percentage point*

(5) Divide the percentage point by *Step 2*

= *percent difference (%)*

(6) Multiply full damages by the percent difference

= *true proportional damages award for loss of chance*

---

[241] *See* Gould, *supra* note 1 (breaking down and showing usefulness of survival distribution).

The above steps are distilled into the following formula:

$$[\left\{\frac{[\ (pre\ negligence) - (post\ negligence)]}{(pre\ negligence)}\right\} \times (100)]\ x\ (full\ damages)^{242}$$

To illustrate how this formula applies in the context of two hypothetical cases, imagine the following:

[1] Mr. Baggins visited a walk-in clinic, complaining of sharp pain below his ribs, radiating from his abdomen to his groin. Mr. Baggins also reported oliguria, weakness, loss of weight, and nausea. Upon physical examination, pitting edema of bilateral extremities was documented, heart rate was 97 *beats per minute* (*not untypical*), blood pressure was 170/94 mm Hg, and respiration was 27 *breaths per minute* (*atypical*). The attending physician ordered both urinalysis and a series of blood tests, which revealed the following: *cadmium* (3.2 μg/g CR); *glycosuria* (*abnormal*); *albumin* (5.5 g/dL); *N-acetyl-beta-D glucosaminidase* (NAG) (7.21 U/g CR); *glomerular filtration rate* (GFR) (45 mL/min/1.73 m²); *Blood Urea Nitrogen* (BUN) (57 mg/dL); *Blood pH* (7.29); CO_2 (20.0 mEq/L); Glucose (161 mg/dL); *Potassium* (4.8 mEq/L); *Calcium* (7.5 mg/dL); and *Chloride* (108 mEq/L); *Sodium* (147 mEq/L). Consequently, despite the signs of nephrotoxicity, the attending physician rendered a diagnosis of diabetes, prescribing Humulin R U-500 (*soluble insulin*), and recommending Mr. Baggins lower his protein intake and exercise daily. Three weeks later,

---

[242] Alvan R. Feinstein, *Invidious Comparisons and Unmet Clinical Challenges*, 92 AM. J. Med. 117 (1992); *Cf.* Lars Noah, *An Inventory of Mathematical Blunders in Applying the Loss-of-A-Chance Doctrine*, 24 Rev. Litig. 369, 394 (2005) (presenting the attributable risk calculation); and Zaven T. Saroyan, *The Current Injustice of the Loss of Chance Doctrine: An Argument for A New Approach to Damages*, 33 Cumb. L. Rev. 15, 36 (2003) (presenting the Relative Proportionality Approach: (.5) x [(the proportion of loss) x (the remaining value of the injured person's life)]). Notably, the Walker Approach to calculating damages was completely created independently from Zaven Saroyan's Relative Proportionality Approach and that of the attributable risk calculation, or approaches that may be deemed similar in any respect (*Feist Publications, Inc. v. Rural Tel. Serv. Co.*, 499 U.S. 340 (1991); 17 U.S.C.A. § 101 (West)); U.S. Const. art. I, § 8, cl. 8). Access and review of these approaches was only obtained years later after the Walker Approach had been formulated. Having since reviewed these approaches, a discussion will follow that distinguishes the Walker Approach from them.

Mr. Baggins presented to the emergency room after fainting on his hike up *Mt. Demise*. While awaiting the attending physician's arrival, Mr. Baggins told the nurse of his recent visit to the walk-in clinic, where they tested his blood and conducted a urinalysis. The nurse informed the attending physician of this information, who thereafter, obtained the results from Mr. Baggins walk-in clinic tests. Upon review of those results and further physical examination, Mr. Baggins was placed on dialysis. Notably, the attending physician questioned Mr. Baggins about his place of work and his exposure to metal, as he was concerned with Mr. Baggins high levels of cadmium (*correlative with chronic exposure*). It was determined Mr. Baggins was ingesting high levels of cadmium *via* habitual thumb-sucking, as he had worn a ring around his thumb for the past 17-years. This "one-ring" was comprised of more than *90% cadmium*, a fact confirmed *via* lab testing. Shortly thereafter, Mr. Baggins passed away.

[2]   Mr. Wick, *an avid user of firearms*, presented to his family physician, complaining of a persistent cough, hemoptysis, chest pain, weakness, loss of weight, wheezing, and dysphonia (*minimal*). Due to Mr. Wick's occupation, the physician knew of his long-time patient's daily exposure to high levels of lead inhalation *via* aerosol discharge upon gun firing. Moreover, the physician knew of Mr. Wick's familial history with laryngeal cancer. Despite this, rather than conduct a laryngoscopy, the physician prescribed lansoprazole to treat what she believed to be *gastroesophageal reflux disease*. Two weeks later, Mr. Wick visited the emergency room, complaining of worsening symptoms. After physical examination was undertaken, a low-dose computerized tomography scan of Mr. Wick's lungs was ordered, in addition to a laryngoscopy. Further, a biopsy was taken and sent to the laboratory for testing. Subsequently, not only was a diagnosis of early-stage laryngeal cancer entered, but so too was that of bronchitis. Unfortunately, Mr. Wick passed away that night due to complications stemming from his bronchial infection.

The estates of both *Mr. Baggins* and *Mr. Wick* filed separate actions against their initial treatment providers. At trial, both initial attending physicians were found to have breached the requisite standard of care owed to their patients. Experts determined that at the time of the initial misdiagnosis, Mr. Baggins had a 40% chance of survival, which by the time of a correct diagnosis, declined to 20%. Comparably, experts at Mr. Wick's trial determined that at the time of the initial misdiagnosis, his chance of survival (*pre-negligence*) was 60%. However, after the family physician's negligence, this value declined to 50%. Full damages, *in both cases*, are assessed at $100,000.

Under the all or nothing approach, Mr. Wick recovers full damages, whereas Mr. Baggins likely will be unable to recover anything.[243] **Under the Walker approach**, Mr. Wick recovers $16,666 and Mr. Baggins recovers $50,000. Arguably, the analysis of the Walker approach offers the most judicious approach, as the damages awarded actually take into account the true amount of chance that was lost.

Appreciably, it would be *illogical* and *injudicious* to allow full recovery to Mr. Wick who suffered a 16.6% decrease in chance in comparison to the 50% decrease Mr. Baggins suffered. Yet, in a number of jurisdictions we continue to preclude recovery, *unless* chance surpasses 50%.[244] However, as I have shown, 50% is an **absolute value**, which mathematically speaking, means nothing in the context of lost chance. As such, a continuum is a poor and truly inappropriate method for assessing loss of chance. Further, to limit Mr. Baggins's recovery to 20% of the full damages and award Mr. Wick the full amount, would seem quite flawed given the actual loss both patients sustained.

---

[243] What would be the result if we apply this scenario to the variants detailed in Exercise: A Relative Analysis in Place of a Threshold One? **Under the first variant**, i.e., *the traditional approach +*, Mr. Wick again recovers full damages, however, Mr. Baggins recovers $20,000. **Under the second variant**, *i.e., pro rata extremus*, Mr. Wick recovers $10,000, and Mr. Baggins recovers $20,000. How do you feel about these results?

[244] *See e.g.*, 2003 CanLII 50091; 836 N.W.2d 321; 126 N.M. 807; 255 Kan. 199; 481 Pa. 256; 146 Haw. 540; 828 S.W.2d 681; 393 N.W.2d 131; 691 A.2d 641; 734 N.E.2d 535; 2003 WY 91, *on reh'g* 2004 WY 44; 107 Nev. 1 (1991); 361 Or. 456; 1987 OK 69; 141 Ariz. 597; 498 So. 2d 713; 452 Mass. 1; 454 Mich. 639; 48 F.Supp.2d 924; and 272 S.W.3d 146.

Consequently, *the Walker Approach* would offer jurisdictions, not only a viable solution for recovery, but an equitable one. Currently, those who argue for proportionate recovery, *via the loss of chance doctrine*, face the challenge of arguing why full damages remain justified once chance surpasses 50%.[245] In other words, where applied, physicians would necessarily face an unfair burden of having to pay full damages where the loss of chance surpasses 50%, while still yet, necessitate proportionate payment in the event chance falls beneath or at such value (the ol' *"damned if you do"* conundrum). *The Walker approach* strips away the flawed continuum upon which loss of chance is assessed and imposes recovery that is *proportionate* to the actual loss. Importantly, "but for" causation could be inserted here, as it can be said that *but for* the physician's negligence Mr. Baggins would not have suffered a 50% loss.

Significantly, the outcome of injury or death, is not a determining factor in this discussion. What is relevant is <u>chance</u>, which is *real* and *tangible*, and when deprived of, should be actionable.[246] This approach would be beneficial to plaintiffs, as any degree of loss is compensable. Accordingly, it would now be the plaintiff's decision as to whether the percent value of the chance lost merits bringing a suit. Notably, physicians should be open to this variant of *the loss of chance doctrine*, as <u>currently</u> where a patient's chance went from 57% to 52% full damages are awarded.[247] This seems unfair to the physician, given the patient, under *the Walker approach*, can only be said to have suffered an 8.77% loss of chance.

Apropos, the Walker approach provides a formula for calculation which is both manageable and easy, and restricts imposition of liability to those defendants, *who through negligence*, were the cause of any loss of chance.

---

[245] 272 S.W.3d at 159 (Noble, J., dissenting).

[246] *Id.* at 161 ("While not physical, the loss of the chance for a better recovery is real, and it resonates with anyone who has ever been denied an opportunity for something important.").

[247] *Id.* ("plaintiff need only show a better than 50% chance in order to recover the full measure of damages against the physician.").

Chapter 14

OTHER ALTERNATIVES?

Notably, the courts inability to value loss of chance appropriately has not gone unnoticed, with some scholars themselves, *as I*, attempting to take a crack at recommending a more *apt* formula for calculating damages. While the approaches below appear to have been confined to resolving such errors in the United States, a review of them is still valuable for any jurisdiction considering whether to adopt the loss of chance doctrine. To appreciate how these approaches function within the realm of medical negligence, imagine the following scenario:

The Black Spot

Mr. Sparrow, an avid seafarer by trade, presented to the emergency room with severe hematochezia and anemia, and contusions (*black spots*). Upon examination, Dr. Swan noted substantial gingival bleeding and hypertrophy. Accordingly, in addition to recommending Mr. Sparrow visit a dentist, Dr. Swan prescribed rectal mesalamine (5-aminosalicylic acid) (*Salofalk*) to treat the hematochezia, and a blood transfusion was carried out to treat Mr. Sparrow's anemic state. Notably, Mr. Sparrow relayed to Dr. Swan that his diet consisted solely of salted pork and rum, and that he had an aversion to anything characterizable as a fruit or vegetable. Not surprisingly, laboratory testing revealed not only low serum concentrations of ascorbic acid, but also of iron, 1,25-hydroxyvitamin D (1,25-OH-vitamin D), 25-hydroxyvitamin D (25-OH-vitamin D), and ferritin. Despite these results, Dr. Swan discharged Mr. Sparrow and recommended he get some rest and take two-weeks off from sailing the open-sea. One-month later, Mr. Sparrow returned to the emergency room after fainting at sea. *In addition to a high fever*, nurse Calypso noted Mr. Sparrow exhibited the following: perifollicular hemorrhage and erythema, subperiosteal hematomas, and follicular hyperkeratosis. Laboratory testing again revealed low serum concentrations of ascorbic acid, iron, 1,25-hydroxyvitamin D (1,25-OH-vitamin D), 25-hydroxyvitamin D (25-OH-vitamin D), and ferritin. Upon both learning of these results and hearing of Mr. Sparrow's inadequate diet, attending physician, Dr. Turner, renders a diagnosis of scurvy and decides to administer ascorbic acid. However, while waiting for the nurse to return to administer the ascorbic acid, Mr. Sparrow has a seizure, and shortly thereafter, dies from an intracerebral hemorrhage (*hemorrhagic stroke*). At trial, medical experts from both sides testify that had Mr. Sparrow's scurvy been treated properly, death more than likely would not have occurred. Despite this, Mr. Sparrow's severe initial condition precluded any of the medical experts from asserting, with complete certainty, Mr. Sparrow would have undoubtedly recovered. Accordingly, the medical experts agree that Mr. Sparrow had an initial 60% chance of survival, which ultimately dropped to 15% thereafter. Damages are valued at $100,000.

What is the correct method of valuation? Having set the pieces, it now becomes possible to explore how other scholars have attempted to remedy the judiciaries' dyscalculia. The default approach of most, as previously shown, is the *all-or-nothing* approach, in which full damages are awarded to those plaintiffs who can show that the physician's negligence was *the more likely than not* (>50%) cause of their injury or death. Consequently, for a *patient-plaintiff* like Mr. Sparrow, such burden would not be arduous, as his initial chance of survival surpassed 50%. Therefore, he would very likely recover full damages. However, assuming the court was compelled to calculate the actual loss of chance Mr. Sparrow sustained, how would they undertake to do so?

Overwhelmingly, court's view Mr. Sparrow's loss from 60% to 15% as a loss of 45 percentage points.[248] Necessarily, as this text has already detailed, this is the wrong result, *for as shown previously*, under the *Walker Approach*, the actual loss suffered would not be 45%, *but rather*, 75%.[249] Notably, this is the result that Justice Dore recognized in *Herskovits v. Grp. Health Co-op. of Puget Sound*, 99 Wash. 2d 609, 619 (1983), despite thereafter incorrectly returning to the percent point figure.[250] Appreciably, even in the concurring

---

[248] *See e.g.*, 580 A.2d at 209 ("For example, if the patient had a 40% chance of recovery and negligent treatment reduced the patient's chance of survival to 10%, then the actual loss of chance of survival would be 30%."); and 741 P.2d at 477 ("To illustrate the method in a case where the jury determines from the statistical findings combined with the specific facts relevant to the patient the patient originally had a 40% chance of cure and the physician's negligence reduced the chance of cure to 25%, (40% − 25%) 15% represents the patient's loss of survival. If the total amount of damages proved by the evidence is $500,000, the damages caused by defendant is 15% x $500,000 or $75,000.").

[249] Alvan R. Feinstein, *Invidious Comparisons and Unmet Clinical Challenges*, 92 AM. J. Med. 117 (1992); *Cf.* Lars Noah, *An Inventory of Mathematical Blunders in Applying the Loss-of-A-Chance Doctrine*, 24 Rev. Litig. 369, 394 (2005) (presenting the attributable risk calculation); and Zaven T. Saroyan, *The Current Injustice of the Loss of Chance Doctrine: An Argument for A New Approach to Damages*, 33 Cumb. L. Rev. 15, 36 (2003) (presenting the Relative Proportionality Approach: (.5) x [(the proportion of loss) x (the remaining value of the injured person's life)]). Notably, the Walker Approach to calculating damages was completely created independently from Zaven Saroyan's Relative Proportionality Approach and that of the attributable risk calculation, or approaches that may be deemed similar in any respect (*Feist Publications, Inc. v. Rural Tel. Serv. Co.*, 499 U.S. 340 (1991); 17 U.S.C.A. § 101 (West)); U.S. Const. art. I, § 8, cl. 8). Access and review of these approaches was only obtained years later after the Walker Approach had been formulated. Having since reviewed these approaches, a discussion will follow that distinguishes the Walker Approach from them.

[250] *Herskovits v. Grp. Health Co-op. of Puget Sound*, 99 Wash. 2d 609, 614 and 619, 664 P.2d 474, 476 and 479 (1983) ("such negligence was the proximate cause of reducing his chances of survival by 14 percent."). Appreciably, even though Justice Dore recognizes that the reduction from 39% to 25% equates to a 36% reduction in the patient's chance of survival, he no less references the loss as 14% throughout the majority opinion. *Id.* at 614 and 610-19.

opinion of *Herskovits* — *for which four judges of the six that encompassed the majority opinion joined* — the incorrect computation of percentage point (*i.e.*, arrived at through simple subtraction) is relied on.[251] *Surprisingly*, two other scholars recognized this valuation of arriving at 75% as appropriate, though *seemingly* and *arguably*, neither were able to correctly apply it thereafter. Specifically, in 1985, Patricia Andel stated in a footnote that the *Herskovits* court's 36% value, not 14%, was correct, yet thereafter, Patricia arguably either incorrectly applies this calculation or fails to appreciate that it differs from the percentage probability test.[252] Similarly, Zaven Saroyan, recognized the appropriate means of valuing loss, but added a multiplier and tied the equation to future earnings.[253] Accordingly, the resulting product is what Saroyan terms the "Relative Proportionality Approach": (.5) x [(the proportion of

---

In fact, the 14% figure is referenced 8 times throughout the opinion, whereas 36% is referenced only once. *Id.* at 610-45.

[251] *Herskovits v. Grp. Health Co-op. of Puget Sound*, 99 Wash. 2d 609, 622, 664 P.2d 474, 480 (1983) (Pearson, J., *concurring*) ("Therefore, the only indications from the record of the extent of the reduction in Mr. Herskovits' chance of long-term survival are that it was "substantial" and that it was at most a 14 percent reduction (from 39 percent to 25 percent)").

[252] Patricia L. Andel, *Comment, Medical Malpractice: The Right to Recover for the Loss of a Chance of Survival*, 12 Pepp. L. Rev. 973, 995 n.104 (1985) ("Referring to the decedent's reduction in chance from 39% to 25%, the court properly recognized that this was a 36% reduction in the decedent's chance of survival, rather than making the common mistake of calculating this reduction as a 14% decrease (as did the medical expert in his testimony), which relates to the physician's degree of causation of the actual death"). According to Lars Noah, Patricia "then immediately failed to apply her own preferred method of calculation. *See id.* at 996-97 (discussing a hypothetical loss of a 40% chance of survival)." Lars Noah, *An Inventory of Mathematical Blunders in Applying the Loss-of-A-Chance Doctrine*, 24 Rev. Litig. 369, 405 n. 20 (2005). However, upon further review of the footnotes, it appears arguably that one of two things is occurring: (1) that Lars is incorrect, as Patricia does in fact state that she is using the method of the equation in n.104, and therefore, Patricia incorrectly applies that equation, arriving at 40%, when she ought to have reached 100% instead; or (2) Patricia mixes apples with oranges, failing to appreciate that the method for computing percent difference is different from percentage probability, as in applying the latter, Patricia arrived at 40%, when she would have reached 100% had she calculated percent difference. Patricia L. Andel, *Comment, Medical Malpractice: The Right to Recover for the Loss of a Chance of Survival*, 12 Pepp. L. Rev. 973, at 995-97 and n.110 (1985). Ultimately, one thing that is clear is that Patricia incorrectly offers the formula utilized to calculate percent difference as an example of an equation using the method in the percentage probability test. *Id.* at 996 n.110.

[253] Zaven Saroyan, *The Current Injustice of the Loss of Chance Doctrine: An Argument for A New Approach to Damages*, 33 Cumb. L. Rev. 15 (2003).

loss) x (the remaining value of the injured person's life)].[254] Thus, despite Mr. Sparrow's chance being reduced by 75%, his damages award would be $37,500, as opposed to the $75,000 awarded under *the Walker Approach.*

Arguably, *while commendable*, the "Relative Proportionality Approach" *undercompensates* plaintiff's in adding a multiplier of .5. Understandably, this result may be more palatable to a jurisdiction that is on the *so-called "fence"* with respect to adopting the loss of chance doctrine, as it cuts the recovery that a *patient-plaintiff* is entitled to in half. However, in doing so, the recovery that the "Relative Proportionality Approach" affords, fails to reflect the very fact that the negligent physician diminished the *patient-plaintiff's* chance in our scenario by 75%. *Indeed*, Saroyan seems to fall short in offering justification as to why loss of chance damages should be cut *in half*, with his addition of a .5 multiplier.[255] Moreover, this approach narrows itself arguably too much, focusing solely on "future earnings," when so much more *ought* to be considered, as detailed in this text earlier.[256]

Notably, Saroyan himself believes his method "falls short of adequately solving the problem."[257] Consequently, *as a solution*, Saroyan suggests that the "Relative Proportionality Approach" be altered to reflect the following formula: (.5) x [(the proportion of loss) x (the inherent value of the person's life)] + (.5) x [(the proportion of loss) x (the remaining value of the injured person's life)].[258] With respect to the former addition, Saroyan submits that "in order to take

---

[254] Zaven Saroyan, *The Current Injustice of the Loss of Chance Doctrine: An Argument for A New Approach to Damages*, 33 Cumb. L. Rev. 15, 36 (2003).

[255] Aside from simply attempting to approximate "the multiplier method previously and consistently used by the courts," no other justification as to why loss of chance recovery ought to be cut in half is seemingly afforded. *Id.* at 37-8.

[256] *Id.* at 38 ("This calculation includes the use of mortality tables (intended to find the average life expectancy of an individual given differing variables) combined with the amount of income that individual would have earned given their present income and often their prospects for advancement.").

[257] *Id.* at 42 n. 189.

[258] *Id.* at 42 n. 189.

this inherent value into account, society should assign a value to each individual, by statute, equal to every other individual."[259] Appreciably, while Saroyan recognizes that Society is not yet ready for an approach such as this (*i.e., where all lives are viewed as equal*), he no less advances it, suggesting that it would increase efficiency and encourage more settlements.[260]

While the merit of such arguments may be debated, such an approach seems to *overcomplicate* things, while also too narrowly focusing on *inherent worth* and *monetary earnings*. After all, *with respect to the former*, why not include a lump sum of damages that reflects both remaining value of life and its inherent value (*notably, one might argue other factors should be added to such list*). *Considerably*, despite this achieving the same result, it would offer a much more *straight-forward* and *less-complex* formula for those trying to "digest" it:

Example # 1
$(.5)\ [(.75 \times \$50,000)] + (.5)\ [(.75 \times 50,000)] = (\$18,750) + (\$18,750)$ $= \$37,500$
Versus
$(.5)\ (.75 \times \$100,000) = \$37,500$

Example # 2
$(.5)\ (.75 \times \$78,289) + (.5)\ (.75 \times \$90,090) = (\$29,358.38) +$ $(\$33,783.75) = \$63,142.13$
Versus
$(.5)\ (.75 \times \$168,379) = \$63,142.13$

Ultimately, *despite its inherent flaws*, it should be acknowledged that the "Relative Proportionality Approach" offers an approach that is "closer" to correctly valuing loss of chance, in

---

[259] *Id.* at 42 n. 189.
[260] *Id.* at 42 n. 189.

comparison to *the proportional damages approach.*[261] To his credit, Saroyan does not make the crucial mistake that so many other scholars and jurisdictions have alike made in valuing chance by *percentage point* (*i.e.*, Sparrow's loss = 45%, not 75%, is incorrect). Further, Saroyan's secondary proposal — (.5) x [(the proportion of loss) x (the inherent value of the person's life)] + (.5) x [(the proportion of loss) x (the remaining value of the injured person's life)] — which seeks to include the inherent value of the *patient-plaintiff's* life (*inherent worth* and *monetary earnings*), exhibits quality in the fact that he suggests it may be used not only where death occurs, but also wherever chance is lost.[262]

ATTRIBUTABLE RISK CALCULATION

Yet another scholar, Lars Noah, has proposed that the attributable risk calculation is the "most appropriate figure to select when resolving these peculiar medical malpractice claims."[263] Notably, *upon a cursory review*, the attributable risk formulation has been presented elsewhere by other scholars *claiming* or *assessing* its viability.[264] Specifically, rather than focus on chance, this approach seeks to place its stock in "risk." Thus, rather than focus on Mr. Sparrow's 75% reduction in his chance of survival, *the attributable risk calculation* seeks to instead, concentrate on the increase in risk that the physician's negligence caused to Sparrow.

Apropos, rather than begin by subtracting Mr. Sparrow's two survival estimates (.60-.15), attributable risk starts by subtracting Mr.

---

[261] It appears as though Saroyan recognizes the flaws of his approach, stating "The method of valuation the author proposes, though admitting its inherent flaws, comes closer to something that is more...." *Id.* at 40.

[262] *Id.* at 42 n. 189.

[263] Lars Noah, *An Inventory of Mathematical Blunders in Applying the Loss-of-A-Chance Doctrine*, 24 Rev. Litig. 369, 378 (2005).

[264] *See e.g.*, Melissa M. Thompson, *Causal Inference in Epidemiology: Implications for Toxic Tort Litigation*, 71 N.C. L. Rev. 247 (1992) (applying attributable risk in the context of toxic tort litigation); and Vern R. Walker, *Direct Interference in the Lost Chance Cases: Factfinding Constraints Under Minimal Fairness to Parties*, 23 Hofstra L. Rev. 247, 307 n. 14 (1994) ("Thus, a point estimate of the relative risk of death from being in the reference situation (with defendant's negligence), as compared to the risk from being in the reference situation but absent the defendant's negligence, is 75 /61 = 1.23.").

Sparrow's two survival estimates from 100%.[265] Consequently, this would leave us with two figures: 40% and 85%, *respectively*.[266] In other words, this speaks to the fact that when Mr. Sparrow first presented to the emergency room, he had a 40% chance of dying. This follows, as *if* Mr. Sparrow had a 60% chance of living when he first arrived in the emergency room, he dually had a 40% chance of succumbing to his scurvy. Likewise, when he later returned to the emergency room, Mr. Sparrow's chance of survival was 15%, and thus, he dually had an 85% chance of death. Notice, all we are doing here is taking the flip-side of the patient's chance of survival.[267]

The next step is to arrive at the *attributable fraction or rate ratio*, the former of which can be achieved *via* taking the 85% risk Sparrow had *following negligence* and subtracting his initial risk of 40% from that value.[268] Thereafter, the value that is achieved is divided by the 85% risk Sparrow had *following negligence*, resulting in an *attributable risk* of 53%.[269] Comparably, the *rate ratio* is obtained *via* taking the 85% risk Sparrow had *following negligence* and dividing that value by his initial risk of 40%.[270] In carrying out such operation, one is able to obtain a *relative risk* of 2.13.[271] All of this to say, since the value falls above 50% (*or 2.13*), the physician's negligence more than likely caused the injury that the *patient-plaintiff* ultimately sustained.[272] In other words, one might argue that since this figure is over the *50% threshold* required under the *preponderance of the evidence* standard, it ought to be accepted as satisfying causation.

Not surprisingly, the attributable risk approach could be of great benefit, enabling plaintiff's to more easily satisfy the

---

[265] Lars Noah, *An Inventory of Mathematical Blunders in Applying the Loss-of-A-Chance Doctrine*, 24 Rev. Litig. 369, 394 (2005).
[266] *Id.*
[267] *Id.* at 395 ("Instead of asking about the loss of a chance for survival, courts should focus on the flip-side question framed as the increased risk of morbidity and mortality.").
[268] *Id.* at 394.
[269] *Id.*
[270] *Id.*
[271] *Id.*
[272] *Id.*

unforgiving threshold of establishing causation. Notably, for a *patient-plaintiff* such as Sparrow, mortality rate was seemingly greater than doubled following the physician's negligence.[273] According to Noah, "[i]t makes more sense to focus on the risk of death before and after the malpractice and ask whether it had more than doubled."[274] To advance his argument, he considers the scenario in which a patient has a 40% chance of survival that decreases to 20% following medical negligence:

> [M]ost courts would find a 20% reduction in the chance of survival--what statisticians call the "rate difference." It makes more sense to focus on the risk of death before and after the malpractice and ask whether it had more than doubled. As the attributable risk and relative risk figures demonstrate, a 20 percentage point increase in the risk of death from 60% to 80% would not come close to satisfying traditional causation requirements. The identical rate difference running from 50% to 70% also would fail $((.70-.50)/.70 = 28.6\%$, or a relative risk of 1.4), but a 20 percentage point increase in the risk of death from 10% to 30% would succeed $((.30-.10)/.30 = 66.7\%$, or a relative risk of 3.0, which represents more than a doubling over the background risk).[275]

In truth, one may find it difficult, *as I do*, to see why such an approach is to be valued, especially since, as Noah proclaims, "[j]udges do not appear to appreciate these differences, and at least one court seemed to get it precisely backwards."[276] Necessarily, in electing to apply the attributable risk method, a *patient-plaintiff* who otherwise suffers a 50% diminution in chance $((.40-.20)/.40)$ ultimately receives no recovery, as the attributable risk of 25% falls well below the 50% threshold of causation. Yet, Noah argues this result still makes more sense:

> Nonetheless, even if they would not award full damages to a

---

[273] Lars Noah, *An Inventory of Mathematical Blunders in Applying the Loss-of-A-Chance Doctrine*, 24 Rev. Litig. 369, 394 (2005).
[274] *Id.* at 398-99.
[275] *Id.*
[276] *Id.* at 399.

patient whose chances of survival declined from, let us say, 99% to 95% and then died, it still makes more sense to convert these figures to the increased risk and award 80% damages $((.05-.01)/.05)$ rather than award only 4% damages based on either the absolute or relative chance lost. Moreover, the way that a court frames the inquiry could have a tremendous impact in jurisdictions that recognize loss-of-a-chance claims but do so asymmetrically-- namely, awarding only proportional damages below 50% but treating the issue as one of causation rather than valuation above the preponderance threshold by allowing full damage awards.[277]

Notably, having previously discussed the *all-or-nothing approach*, we know that the *patient-plaintiff* Noah describes would in reality, likely receive full compensation (*assuming negligence is shown*), as his initial chance of survival sat well above the 50% threshold needed to establish causation.[278] Recall, *the Walker Approach*, rather than award full damages, would enable this *patient-plaintiff* to recover 4% of the damages $((.99-.95)/.99)$, as such result reflects the actual diminution in chance that the individual suffered. However, Noah asserts that it is more logical to award 80% of the damages instead, as this award reflects the value by which the *patient-plaintiff's* risk of death was increased $((.05-.01)/.05)$.[279] Thus, *the question must be asked*, which approach gets it right?

---

[277] Lars Noah, *An Inventory of Mathematical Blunders in Applying the Loss-of-A-Chance Doctrine*, 24 Rev. Litig. 369, 399–400 (2005).

[278] 272 S.W.3d at 161 (Noble, J., dissenting) ("plaintiff need only show a better than 50% chance in order to recover the full measure of damages against the physician.").

[279] Lars Noah, *An Inventory of Mathematical Blunders in Applying the Loss-of-A-Chance Doctrine*, 24 Rev. Litig. 369, 399 (2005).

THE WALKER APPROACH V. ATTRIBUTABLE RISK

Arguably, it seems that applying the attributable risk approach fails to fix the problem, *overcompensating* and *undercompensating* the individuals it seeks to aid. For instance, *as recited previously*, Noah uses the following scenario to demonstrate that the attributable risk approach makes more sense:

> As the attributable risk and relative risk figures demonstrate, a 20 percentage point increase in the risk of death from 60% to 80% would not come close to satisfying traditional causation requirements. The identical rate difference running from 50% to 70% also would fail $((.70-.50)/.70 = 28.6\%$, or a relative risk of 1.4), but a 20 percentage point increase in the risk of death from 10% to 30% would succeed $((.30-.10)/.30 = 66.7\%$, or a relative risk of 3.0, which represents more than a doubling over the background risk).[280]

Ironically, such results seem *nonsensical*, as it would fail to afford any recovery for two of the three plaintiff's Noah presents, while arguably undercompensating the third *patient-plaintiff*. *With respect to the latter*, it would be futile for a *patient-plaintiff* to demonstrate a 66.7% attributable risk in order to obtain 66.7% of the damages, as they already can obtain full damages through *the traditional standard*.[281] This follows, as the plaintiff's initial chance of survival was 90%, a value well above the 50% threshold imposed by a number of courts and jurisdictions *alike*.[282]

Comparably, in applying *the Walker Approach*, the results achieved through *the attributable risk approach* seem truly illogical, as despite suffering a 22.2% loss of chance $((.90-.70)/.90)$, *the attributable risk approach* would award arguably more recovery than is owed (*i.e.*, 66.7%), whilst failing to compensate those two plaintiffs

---

[280] Lars Noah, *An Inventory of Mathematical Blunders in Applying the Loss-of-A-Chance Doctrine*, 24 Rev. Litig. 369, 398–99 (2005).

[281] *Note*: It is assumed that the *patient-plaintiff* would receive 66.7% of the damages, rather than full damages, as Noah states in the preceding paragraph he would award 80% of the damages. *Id.* at 399.

[282] *See* 272 S.W.3d at 161 (Noble, J., dissenting) ("plaintiff need only show a better than 50% chance in order to recover the full measure of damages against the physician.").

who suffered a 50% and 40% loss of chance *respectively*. *To elaborate*, with respect to those two latter plaintiffs, no recovery would be afforded, as the attributable risks would be deemed 25% ((.80-.60)/.80) and 28.6% ((.70-.50)/.70), both well below the 50% threshold required to establish causation.[283] This seems unjust, as *the Walker Approach* would afford 50% recovery ((.40-.20)/.40) and 40% recovery ((.50-.30)/.50) *respectively*. Thus, where *the Walker Approach* seeks to <u>correctly</u> carry out the aims of the loss of chance doctrine, affording *proportionate recovery* to those plaintiffs who sustained a negligent diminution in chance, the attributable risk approach fails to accomplish such ends.

In the end, Noah argues that the method *the Walker Approach* employs produces absurd results.[284] To substantiate this, he contends that where a *patient-plaintiff* suffers a diminution in chance of survival from 2% to 0%, or 14% to 0%, it would be a serious error to award 100% of the damages.[285] Yet, *in that same breath*, Noah asserts that a patient who suffers a 100% to 90% diminution in chance should be afforded <u>complete</u> recovery (*limited to where the ultimate outcome occurs*), as the patient's attributable risk would be 100% ((.10-0)/.10).[286]

One may be truly confounded by the logic of these arguments, *as on one hand*, Noah awards full damages to an individual who: (1) already would have received full damages under *the traditional approach* and (2) only suffered a 10% loss of chance ((1-.90)/1); *while on the other hand*, refuses to award those same damages to two individuals who suffered a 100% diminution in chance ((((.02-0)/.02) *and* ((.14-0)/.14)).[287]

---

[283] Noah, *supra* note 279.
[284] *Id.* at 402-03.
[285] *Id.*
[286] *Id.*
[287] *Id.*

ALEA IACTA EST

Considerably, one thing that should stand out here is the attributable risk approach's failure to appreciate how significant the stakes are when a patient has a 2% chance of life and relies on (*and trusts*) a physician who then performs negligently. Yet, the *attributable risk* approach, as shown immediately above, would award this individual *nothing*, as the attributable risk would be merely 2% ((1-.98)/1). Necessarily, *the Walker Approach* manages to capture these realities, awarding *just* and *fair* compensation to <u>both</u> individuals, rather than full damages to one, and nothing to the other.

Ultimately, *as Noah recognizes*, how one frames the injury, either as one of *loss of chance* or *increase in risk*, can be of paramount consequence when it comes to realizing the amount of damages that may be awarded.[288] While Noah adopts the position that increase in risk affords the *apt* perspective, one may argue, *as I do*, that such focus is too narrow.[289]

This follows, as should one necessarily frame the analysis as one of increase in risk, one is then immediately forced to determine whether the ultimate outcome was in fact sustained. For the two are so inextricably bound, that separating either one would produce *irrational* results. Necessarily, I find it hard to imagine that physicians would be accepting of an approach wherein which culpability is assigned not on death or injury suffered, but on mere increase in risk. *A fortiori*, the same would more than likely be true for those scholars and jurisdictions who are already "uncomfortable" with the notion of holding physicians liable for a reduction in chance where the ultimate outcome has yet to manifest.

Thus, *arguably, the attributable risk approach* must be confined solely to those cases where death or injury occurs. Consequently, this has a limiting effect that is <u>unfound</u> in *the Walker Approach*, which views chance as a *distinct injury*, regardless of

---

[288] Lars Noah, *An Inventory of Mathematical Blunders in Applying the Loss-of-A-Chance Doctrine*, 24 Rev. Litig. 369, 394–97 and 404 (2005).
[289] *Id.*

whether the ultimate outcome manifests itself. Notably, framing injury in terms of loss of chance ought to focus one on something that is tangible... *something that is lost*.[290] In contrast, simply because a physician increases their patient's risk of death, does not mean that patient suffered any resultant harm. However, if that same physician denied their patient a chance, that constitutes something that *is real*.[291] This is actual loss and damage, *for in that diminution*, the physician denied you more than just a chance to recover and survive, but the chance to set your affairs in order, to seek better treatment or alternative treatment, to manage symptoms and end suffering, *etc*. *Arguably*, all of this gets *thrown out of the window* when one focuses solely on the increase in risk.

Appreciably, while one might assert this is purely a manner of semantics, the reality still stands, *chance is meaningful*. Perhaps, one may even be so bold to contend that less "Physician Dissonance" is achieved through *the Walker Approach*, as physician's, *with respect to loss of chance matters*, can take solace in knowing they will only be held liable for the *actual harm* they cause, *not an increase in risk*, nor full damages where initial chance surpassed an arbitrary threshold.

> "Probability of causation is unfortunate terminology because the attributable risk proportion, without more, does not prove causation and generally may not be extrapolated to the individual."[292]

One more proposal — Interestingly, while the above proposals offer varying levels of recovery, none offer a mechanism which sets out to provide solely full compensation irrespective of whether chance was above or below 50%. *Concordantly*, inspired by the Great Myth of *Tantalus*, I set out to craft such an approach, which I detail below.

---

[290] See 272 S.W.3d at 161 (Noble, J., dissenting) ("Every patient in this scenario doubtless feels that a tangible thing has been lost when they are denied their chance for a better result.").
[291] *Id.* ("While not physical, the loss of the chance for a better recovery is real, and it resonates with anyone who has ever been denied an opportunity for something important.").
[292] Melissa M. Thompson, *Causal Inference in Epidemiology: Implications for Toxic Tort Litigation*, 71 N.C. L. Rev. 247, 252 n.32 (1992).

THE TANTALUS ALTERNATIVE APPROACH

[And so] Zeus cast his son Tantalus into the underworld... [where] Tantalus lived out an existence of interminable frustration...plunged to his neck in a pool of cool water, but every time he tried to drink, the water would recede. Above him branches of ripe fruit hovered just out of his grasp.[293]

I now submit an alternative approach, not purely a loss of chance approach, but rather a separate tort action. Here, double recovery is available to the plaintiff in establishing causal negligence through the "but for" test, and as well, through this alternative approach. Notably, recovery *via* each approach singularly is also possible.

Apropos, I propose introducing the *Tantalus Alternative Test*, a modified objective test within which loss of chance would operate. Specifically, this test assesses whether a reasonable person in the patient's position would have forgone the prescribed treatment and instead pursued actualization of the chance, *if correctly diagnosed. Necessarily, the Tantalus Alternative Test* would not circumvent *nor* nullify causation, rather it would merely restructure and render it suitable for the given circumstances. Ergo, the patient must still establish causation on a *preponderance of the evidence* (*equiv. balance of probabilities*).

Notably, this test is a variant of the *informed consent test* applied by the Supreme Court in *Reibl v. Hughes*, [1980] 2 SCR 880, where the Court recognized an exception to the "but for" test was

---

[293] Robert Goff, *Tantalizing Tantalus*, Forbes (Feb. 23, 1998)
https://www.forbes.com/forbes/1998/0223/6104154a.html?sh=db747d1306c7.

warranted, specific to matters of informed consent.[294] However, in cases of negligent misdiagnosis, the value of informed consent is irrelevant, as consent was given to treatment which proved to be, *for lack of a better word*, incorrect. Instead, my *Tantalus Alternative Test* is concerned with two fundamental elements which flow from a *patient-plaintiff's* right to be competently diagnosed:

(1) the right to not be subjected to incorrect treatment, *and*

(2) the right to actualize the relevant chance.

These two elements are broken down into multiple *non-exhaustive* factors to be considered by the court, such as *quality of life, loss of chance, psychological harm, and pain and suffering*. Here, loss of chance includes not only the *patient-plaintiff's* loss of actualizing their chance at survival, but also the chance to set their affairs and house in order, pursue, *if necessary*, medical assistance in dying, and ease quality of life, *etc.*

Consequently, it is for the court to first apply the *modified objective test*, and once satisfied, it is for the *patient-plaintiff* to establish any of the subjective factors above. Necessarily, where the first part of the *Tantalus Alternative Test* satisfies causation, the second part offers the plaintiff the chance to establish the resultant impact of the negligence; and each factor presented is to be established on a *preponderance of the evidence* (*equiv. balance of probabilities*), or inferred at the discretion of the court. Additionally, the second part of the *Tantalus Alternative Test* allows the court to justify a full damages award, as each factor *combined* provides substantial evidence of the wrong committed and significant justification for full recovery.

Alternatively, if one is concerned that the *Tantalus Alternative Test* establishes an exception to the "but for" test, it may be framed as such: Whether a reasonable person in the *patient-plaintiff's* position would not have elected to follow the treatment prescribed, and instead, pursued actualization of the chance *but for* the physician's negligence.

---

[294] *Reibl v. Hughes*, [1980] 2 SCR 880.

Ultimately, while my *Tantalus Alternative Test* is extreme, it no less affords an additional proposal to those jurisdictions who may be searching for something more to resolve the burdens placed on *patient-plaintiffs* by causal uncertainty. Conversely, for those jurisdictions that feel hesitant to try something so radically different, the Walker Approach, *I believe*, offers a *balanced* and *viable* method.

Looking ahead — in the next chapter we explore how scholars and members of the judiciary have often debated whether chance has *actual value*. Where one person says yes, another says no, and where one takes it as a *matter of fact*, the other takes the opposite as a *matter of fact*. Amidst the cacophony of assertions, how does one determine who is right, and who is *ultimately* wrong?

Chapter 15

WHO'S RIGHT, WHO'S WRONG

Unequivocally, for those jurisdictions who have opted to relegate the loss of chance doctrine into a state of obsolescence, *or those who merely remain betwixt and between*, the predominant issue (*supreme to any and all foci*), is understanding that chance — whether above or below 50% — <u>has value</u> in the context of medical negligence. To better understand this <u>real value</u>, suppose the following:

400 people are diagnosed with colorectal cancer:
>» In Group A, 78 of 100 will survive;
>» In Group B, 60 of 100 will survive;
>» In Group C, 10 of 100 will survive; and
>» in Group D, 5 of 100 will survive.

Hypothetically, if <u>You</u> were in Group A, what *monies* would someone in Group B have to pay you to trade places? Appreciably, I believe it is agreeable that Group A, *without a shadow of a doubt*, has the best chances of survival. *Ergo*, the rational answer to this hypothetical query of which I have put forth to <u>You</u>, is that no amount of *monies* would suffice to impel you to trade places with a member of Group B.

Similarly, *I ask*, if <u>You</u> were in Group C, what *monies* would a Group D patient have to pay you to switch places with them? *Again, and appreciably*, the <u>rational</u> answer is: no amount of *monies* would justify trading places with a member of Group D.[295] Conversely, any amount of monies would be worth switching from Group B to Group A. *However*, for some reason, when presented with similar scenarios, courts are unable (*or unwilling*) to recognize the value of chance other than that above 50%. Necessarily, one might be better served in resolving this difference of opinion by exploring what makes something *true*.[296]

"The opposite of a fact is a falsehood, but the opposite of one profound truth may very well be another profound truth."
– Niels Bohr

Take for instance, the statement: "One nanometer is a billionth of a meter, or 10^{-9} of a meter."[297] This is a matter of scientific fact. *In light of this*, in my other book, *Nano-Bots, Doctors in Disguise: Exploring Loss of Chance at the Nano-Level* (2022), I am able to offer the following fact as a matter of scientific truth:

"If Tolkien's 'One Ring of Power' were a nanometer, then one meter would be the size of the Earth."[298]

---

[295] Andrew M. Palmer, *Kemper v. Gordon: The Kentucky Supreme Court Forecloses the Loss-of-Chance Doctrine in Medical-Malpractice Cases*, 48 U. Louisville L. Rev. 639 (2010) (Notably, these "rational" answers are comparable to those proffered by students of Professor David Leibson, upon his presenting of a similar scenario).

[296] Analysis informed and based on that presented by amspencer1984, *Quote of the week: The Opposite of a Profound Truth, Niels Bohr*, LifeThinkBlog (March 8, 2013), https://lifethinkblog.wordpress.com/2013/03/08/quote-of-the-week-the-opposite-of-a-profound-truth-niels-bohr/.

[297] *What Is Nanotechnology?* Nat'l Nanotech. Initiative, https://www.nano.gov/nanotech-101/what/definition (last visited Apr. 12, 2022) ("One nanometer is a billionth of a meter, or 10^{-9} of a meter.").

[298] *See* Matthew Calloway Walker, *Nano-Bots, Doctors in Disguise: Exploring Loss of Chance at the Nano-Level* (2022); and *Id.*

Could you reasonably debate this fact with me? Not very likely, as if you accept the truth that a nanometer is 10^{-9} of a meter, then you must also accept the premise I offer in turn. In other words, one can confirm whether or not this is true *via* measurement *and of course extrapolation. This is a fact.*

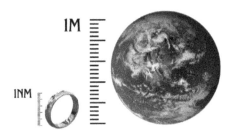

What about this statement: Love is great? How can we determine the validity of this statement? What is love? How might one define it? From a purely neurobiological standpoint, love amounts merely to a by-product of oxytocin, vasopressin, dopamine, and serotonergic signaling, paired with endorphin and endogenous morphinergic mechanisms tied to nitric oxide autoregulatory pathways.[299] Conversely, from an *abstract standpoint*, for some, love is more than just the inner workings of neurobiology, but a feeling captured in the phrases "You had me at hello," "As you wish," "I know," and "Always."[300] It knows no bounds and is a feeling recognized universally. Yet, can its value be measured?

Arguably, while others may protest differently, many may view love as immeasurable. But does this mean that no truth can be subscribed to the statement that love is great? Appreciably, love is great. *Yet, still some may argue that love is terrible*. Is this statement true? Ask anyone who has ever had their heart broken or lost a loved one.

---

[299] Tobias Esch & George B. Stefano, *The Neurobiology of Love*, Neuro Endocrinol Lett. 2005 Jun;26(3):175-92. PMID: 15990719.
[300] Jerry Maguire (1996); The Princess Bride (1987); The Empire Strikes Back (1980); and Harry Potter and the Deathly Hallows: Part II (2011).

Consequently, it can be true that love is great while also true that love is terrible without the very fabric of our reality crumbling before us. *Better phrased, the opposite of one profound truth, is yet another profound truth.*

Ultimately, the same may be said for chance, such that one may argue chance has value above 50%, while another may argue that chance *dually* has value under 50%. *Perhaps*, both statements comprise profound truths. But, to discount either one, would be to confuse either statement with that of a *fact*, the opposite of which is a falsehood. Accordingly, this text has not only demonstrated and provided herein a mechanism that would appropriately value chance, but has *additionally* advanced arguments recognizing what chance may mean to any given patient, *above or below 50%.*

Appreciably, jurisdictions ought to appreciate that simply because they find truth in chance being valuable above 50%, does not mean the same cannot hold truth with respect to chance falling below 50%. Necessarily, while I subscribe to the belief that chance has real tangible value, *no matter how small*, the door is certainly left open for others to counter this belief.

Notably, under *the Walker Approach*, it is not about reprimanding a negligent physician, but rather appreciating the impact that a loss of chance has on a particular patient. While it seems quite convenient to assert that the doctrine would allow those to claim awards where no harm accrued, *but for the diminution in chance*, no scholar seems to have quipped with the realities that the typical patients in these cases face…

…. it is always easier to say something has no value, when we ourselves do not bear the burdens of those who would deem otherwise.

OUT OF THE FRYING PAN & INTO THE FIRE?

A Fox, swimming across a river, was barely able to reach the bank, where he lay bruised and exhausted from his struggle with the swift current. Soon a swarm of blood-sucking flies settled on him; but he lay quietly, still too weak to run away from them. A Hedgehog happened by. "Let me drive the flies away," he said kindly. "No, no!" exclaimed the Fox, "do not disturb them! They have taken all they can hold. If you drive them away, another greedy swarm will come and take the little blood I have left." Better to bear a lesser evil than to risk a greater in removing it.[301]

So much *wanton* fear and worry, *needlessly spent*, has plagued the debate surrounding the adoption of the loss of chance doctrine. Much like *Aesop's Fox*, such arguments have leant themselves to "fear appeals" proclaiming the profound impacts that the loss of chance doctrine will have on *physicians — from insurance premiums to defensive medicine —* while others have focused on the issues inherent in awarding *patient-plaintiffs* recourse where the "ultimate harm" has yet to accrue.

---

[301] *The Aesop for Children*, Library of Congress, *adapted from The Aesop for Children: with Pictures by Milo Winter*, (Rand, McNally & Co. 1919), https://read.gov/aesop/114.html.

However, as detailed previously *herein*, concern over the complexity in applying this doctrine, and fear that the floodgates will open, *thus burdening physicians and courts*, is inherently unsubstantiated.[302]

Consequently, one need no longer prognosticate as to the effects of adopting this doctrine, *but rather*, simply take the time to look at any one, *if not all*, of the 26 states that have already adopted it in some form.[303] Such practice of observation would certainly not be beyond the purview of jurisdictions. *For instance*, the Supreme Court of Canada — unlike its decision in *Rodriguez v. British Columbia (AG)*, [1993] 3 SCR 519 — ruled in *Carter v. Canada (AG)*, 2015 SCC 5 that assisted dying was legal.[304] Notably, this Court in *Carter v. Canada* had the benefit of two decades having passed since deciding *Rodriguez*.[305] Appreciably, this offered the benefit of observing other international jurisdictions' application of assisted suicide.

---

[302] *See e.g.*, Andrew M. Palmer, *Kemper v. Gordon: The Kentucky Supreme Court Forecloses the Loss-of-Chance Doctrine in Medical-Malpractice Cases*, 48 U. Louisville L. Rev. 646-652 (2010) (Analyzing the decision in *Kemper v. Gordon*, 272 S.W.3d 146 (Ky. 2008) to reject the loss of chance doctrine, and showing that the Court's justifications were disputable and debatable); 836 N.W.2d at 349 n. 14; Steven R. Koch, *Whose Loss Is It Anyway? Effects of the "Lost-Chance" Doctrine on Civil Litigation and Medical Malpractice Insurance*, 88 N.C. L. Rev. 595, at 619-27 and 626-30 (2010); and *Fennell v. S. Maryland Hosp. Ctr., Inc.*, 320 Md. 776, 797, 580 A.2d 206, 216 (1990) (Adkins, J., dissenting) ("The elitist notion that Maryland juries would be unable to cope with loss of chance evidence...surely would surprise those who adopted the second paragraph of Article 23 of our Declaration of Rights.").

[303] 836 N.W.2d 321; *Alberts v. Schultz*, 126 N.M. 807 (1999); *Delaney v. Cade*, 255 Kan. 199, 218 (1994); *Hamil v. Bashline*, 481 Pa. 256 (1978); *Est. of Frey v. Mastroianni*, 146 Haw. 540 (2020); *Wollen v. DePaul Health Ctr.*, 828 S.W.2d 681 (Mo. 1992); *DeBurkarte v. Louvar*, 393 N.W.2d 131 (Iowa 1986); *Ferrell v. Rosenbaum*, 691 A.2d 641 (D.C. 1997); *Cahoon v. Cummings*, 734 N.E.2d 535 (Ind. 2000); *McMackin v. Johnson Cnty. Healthcare Ctr.*, 2003 WY 91 (Wyo. 2003), *on reh'g* 2004 WY 44 (Wyo. 2004); *Perez v. Las Vegas Med. Ctr.*, 107 Nev. 1 (1991); *Smith v. Providence Health & Servs.-Oregon*, 361 Or. 456 (2017); *McKellips v. Saint Francis Hosp., Inc.*, 1987 OK 69 (1987); *Thompson v. Sun City Cmty. Hosp., Inc.*, 141 Ariz. 597 (1984); *Hastings v. Baton Rouge Gen. Hosp.*, 498 So. 2d 713 (La. 1986); Fangrow, *supra* note 3; Guest, *supra* note 3; and Charles Jones et al., *"The Loss of Chance" Doctrine in Medical Malpractice Cases*, Troutman Pepper (Mar. 13, 2013), www.troutman.com/insights/the-loss-of-chance-doctrine-in-medical-malpractice-cases.html.

[304] *Rodriguez v. British Columbia (AG)*, [1993] 3 SCR 519; and *Carter v. Canada (AG)*, 2015 SCC 5, 1 SCR 331.

[305] 2015 SCC 5.

In discussing the value of looking to these other jurisdictions, this Court stated the following in *Carter*:

> "Together, these regimes have produced a body of evidence about the practical and legal workings of physician-assisted death and the efficacy of safeguards for the vulnerable."[306]

Comparably, the Supreme Courts of any jurisdiction, *or any lower court for that matter*, would have more than enough applicable evidence from previous cases in the United States, where the loss of chance doctrine has been applied. Necessarily, these cases could be relied on in judging any residual effects from the application of this doctrine and any viable methods relating to its introduction.

THE WALKER APPROACH

TWO CENTS

Ultimately, for any jurisdiction considering adopting the loss of chance doctrine, a number of proposals as presented herein may be acceptable (*math aside*). *Importantly*, although the *Tantalus Alternative test* I have crafted offers arguably the most *plaintiff-friendly* approach, I believe my other approach, *the Walker approach*, offers the one that is the most balanced. But of course, the effective and efficient utilization of any proposal is dependent on the views of both courts and legislatures.

---

[306] *Id.*

"Condemnant quo non Intellegunt"

What is a legal system, if not a renderer of services, adequately framed so as to be a portal *via* which laws are *penned*, numerically ordered and arranged, deciphered, and imposed and protected?[307] Justice is the *quintessential* phenomenon, which lay at the very core of such services rendered. Essentially, there exists a stark *duality* within such core, through which justice is both the means and end, bringing balance to a metaphysical scale. However, does such a scale, as professed, balanced in light *against* dark, blind to bias, and precluded from the proclivity to emerge as corrupt, truly exist? Perhaps, to the extent where it typifies a categorical imperative of the law, justice by and of itself necessitates a *Kantian universality*.

Ultimately, the framing of the interpretation of justice overbearingly influences how decisions are rendered.[308] Metaphorically, this framing is the colander through which information is filtered. The portion of that information remaining in the colander *post-filtration* is that portion which forms our concept of justice to be utilized so long as it aligns with our framing of the case.

---

[307] *The Canadian Legal System*, The Canada Guide, https://thecanadaguide.com/basics/legal-system/.
[308] *See e.g.*, 452 Mass. 1; 272 S.W.3d 146; [1991] 1 SCR 541; [2005] UKHL 2; and 2003 CanLII 50091.

Consequently, how a court chooses to frame its approach to a case will ultimately influence how justice is rendered.

Unfortunately, to be a *patient-plaintiff* today in most jurisdictions is *akin* to "a kite dancing in a hurricane."[309] Take Canada for instance, statistically, out of 100 medical negligence cases, 55.2 will be dismissed, discontinued, or abandoned, 36.7 will be settled, 6.5 will be judgments found in favor of the physician, with only 1.6 of judgments going to the patient.[310]

Importantly, my analysis throughout this paper does not attempt to favor *patients-plaintiffs* over the *physician-defendants*. I recognize physicians are fundamentally dedicated to protecting and improving the health of their patients, committing their time, energy, and resources in this pursuit. Hence, my analysis is confined to only those physicians who have been proved to be negligent.

---

[309] John Logan, *Spectre*, Scripts, http://www.scripts.com/script-pdf/18640 (last visited Aug. 26, 2022).

[310] Habiba Nosheen & Andrew Culbert, *As fewer patients sue their doctor, the rate of winning malpractice suits is dropping too*, CBC (Apr. 18, 2019), www.cbc.ca/news/health/medical-malpractice-doctors-lawsuits-canada-1.4913960 (*note*: these statistics span from 2013-2017 and it is assumed that they have not changed significantly since then); *See also* Douglas Danner, *1 Med. Malprac. Chklsts. & Disc. §* *1:11*, Westlaw (database updated Sept. 2021) ("Statistics show that 95% of all medical malpractice cases are dropped, settled or otherwise disposed of before trial. Of the 5% which go to trial, the defendants win about half of these cases."); and Adam C. Schaffer, et al., *Rates and Characteristics of Paid Malpractice Claims Among US Physicians by Specialty*, 1992-2014, JAMA Intern Med. 717 (2017).

"Ah, Nothing is too late, till the tired heart shall cease to palpitate."
— Henry Wadsworth Longfellow

Chapter 16

END GAME

To conclude, I offer this failure to provide recovery, *as noted herein*, results in a drastic imbalance between *patient* and *physician*. Accordingly, my own proposals that I offer *herein* are characterizable as *deontological* and *teleological* based. Necessarily, an underlying goal of this text is to present loss of chance proposals which any jurisdiction could apply to **re-balance** medical negligence. *Understandably*, here, my reasoning is concern that causation in medical negligence will be condemned — *in line with Justice Binnie's analogy* — to "resemble a voyage of the Flying Dutchman...with no set destination and no end in sight."[311]

Wholeheartedly and sincerely, I hope that my discussion outlined and contained *herein* will prove to be illuminating and stimulating, while at the same time, demonstrate my purest intentions of remaining *dispassionate* and *unbiased* in any one direction toward either *plaintiff* or *defendant*.

---

[311] Lax Kw'alaams Indian Band v. Canada (AG), 2011 SCC 56, 3 SCR 535.

Consequently, the statistics presented *herein*, in addition to the body of case law concerning medical negligence, only underline the need for exacting court parameters that more judicially result in **both** *plaintiff* and *defendant* reaching levels of relative satisfaction… a mandate all courts continually strive to achieve. *Unreservedly*, I thank you greatly for investing your time in reading this text and learning about a topic of which I have gleaned much information through great energy and obsession, having dedicated a significant number of years to researching.

At World's End, I leave you with the following sentiment to *mull* over…

"If the only tool you have is a hammer, you tend to treat everything as if it were a nail."
– A. Maslow

ABOUT THE AUTHOR

MATTHEW CALLOWAY WALKER

Matthew Calloway Walker is a *Dual Juris Doctor*, possessing two law degrees, one from the U.S. and one from Canada, having graduated from both the University of Ottawa Faculty of Law and Michigan State University College of Law (MSU GPA: 3.8 | *Magna Cum Laude* | Class Rank 29 of 230). *Notably*, Matthew is the President, Chair, and Founder of the Walker Health Law Moot, a well-respected competition, that provides law students with the chance to strengthen their advocacy skills and display their talents before over 100 prominent legal and medical professionals from across the U.S. and Canada. This past year, over 600 people attended the event, and over 90 students across eight law schools applied to gain entrance to compete, with spots filling up in less than 60 seconds. The event has raised over $26,000 for those competing, with sponsors such as *McDonalds, Red Bull, LexisNexis, Thomson Reuters, TD Bank, MADD, Michigan State University, The Canadian Bar Association, and several prominent firms.*

Matthew has devoted much of his time to academic scholarship and community involvement. For instance, Matthew has acted as President of the Health Law Students' Association, *a 400+ membered organization*; volunteered with Pro Bono Ontario, *taking on a managerial role for a time therein*; served as liaison for the *dual juris doctorate* program (Canadian Legal Association); collaborated with medical students, as Vice President of Research & Ethics and Vice President of Communications at the NORTH Clinic, to connect marginalized populations to needed services in the community; and competed in the Borden Ladner Gervais Negotiation Competition, the Weiler Mediation Competition, and went to Toronto to represent the University of Ottawa at the 2020 National Bowman Tax Moot.

In 2021, Michigan State University awarded Matthew the Jurisprudence Achievement Award, in recognition of his achievement in the study of law, having been deemed the highest achieving student in his course. Additionally, Matthew was nominated for Laurier's Young Alumnus of the Year award, where prior to law school, he completed his BA studying Psychology & Health Sciences. As an undergraduate, he investigated health related statistics for the aging population in hopes of building a database, and also established a campaign aimed at preventing driving under the influence, amassing 1800 followers. In 2018, Laurier awarded Matthew the Alumni Bronze Medal for the Faculty of Science.

Matthew previously worked at a leading firm in Canada, where he conducted copyright law related work for a major Hollywood studio, reviewed contracts and agreements for large and significant financial transactions, and conducted extensive legal research for a variety of matters, providing insight on crypto, tax, privacy, and bankruptcy related issues, as well as providing risk assessments and policy recommendations. Matthew was also selected to be in the 2020 NBA Draft, as an early entrant.

"Betimes, our paths are laid before us by powers greater than our own. In those moments, it's our task to make our feet go where our hearts wish not to tread."
— *The Stranger*

Thank You

ANALYTICAL TABLE OF CONTENTS

151

Endnotes

i.   *See* Stephen Jay Gould, *The Median Isn't the Message*, 15 Am. Assoc. J. Ethics 77, 77-81 (2013).

ii. *See, e.g.*, Habiba Nosheen & Andrew Culbert, *As fewer patients sue their doctor, the rate of winning malpractice suits is dropping too*, CBC (Apr. 18, 2019), www.cbc.ca/news/health/medical-malpractice-doctors-lawsuits-canada-1.4913960; Douglas Danner, *1 Med. Malprac. Chklsts. & Disc. § 1:11*, Westlaw (database updated Sept. 2021) ("Statistics show that 95% of all medical malpractice cases are dropped, settled or otherwise disposed of before trial. Of the 5% which go to trial, the defendants win about half of these cases."); Adam C. Schaffer, et al., *Rates and Characteristics of Paid Malpractice Claims Among US Physicians by Specialty*, 1992-2014, JAMA Intern Med. 717 (2017).

iii. Paul Fangrow, *Will Loss of Chance Doctrine Lose its Chance in North Carolina?*, Wake Forest Law Review: Current   Issues   Blog   (Sept.   10,   2019), http://www.wakeforestlawreview.com/2019/09/will-loss-of-chance-doctrine-lose-its-chance-in-north-carolina/; Lauren Guest et al., *The "Loss of Chance" Rule As A Special Category of Damages in Medical Malpractice: A State-by-State Analysis*, 21-APR J. Legal Econ. 53 (2015); *Dickhoff ex rel. Dickhoff v. Green*, 836 N.W.2d 321, 344 (Minn. 2013); and *Matsuyama v. Birnbaum*, 452 Mass. 1, 10 (2008), *abrogated by Doull v. Foster*, 487 Mass. 1 (2021).

iv. Joan F. Renehan, *A New Frontier: The Loss of Chance Doctrine in Medical Malpractice Cases*, 53-JUN Boston B.J. 14, 15 (2009); Guest, *supra* note 3; 836 N.W.2d at 344; 452 Mass. at 10; *Cottrelle v. Gerrard*, 2003 CanLII 50091 (ON CA); *Laferrière v. Lawson*, 1991 CanLII 87 (SCC); *Gregg v. Scott*, [2005] UKHL 2; and Harold Luntz, *Loss of Chance in Medical Negligence*, Uni. Mel. Law Sch. Leg. Studies Res. Pap. Ser. (2011).

v.   *Supra* note 3.

vi. 836 N.W.2d 321; *Alberts v. Schultz*, 126 N.M. 807 (1999); *Delaney v. Cade*, 255 Kan. 199, 218 (1994); *Hamil v. Bashline*, 481 Pa. 256 (1978); *Est. of Frey v. Mastroianni*, 146 Haw. 540 (2020); *Wollen v. DePaul Health Ctr.*, 828 S.W.2d 681 (Mo. 1992); *DeBurkarte v. Louvar*, 393 N.W.2d 131 (Iowa 1986); *Ferrell v. Rosenbaum*, 691 A.2d 641 (D.C. 1997); *Cahoon v. Cummings*, 734 N.E.2d 535 (Ind. 2000); *McMackin v. Johnson Cnty. Healthcare Ctr.*, 2003 WY 91 (Wyo. 2003), *on reh'g* 2004 WY 44 (Wyo. 2004); *Perez v. Las Vegas Med. Ctr.*, 107 Nev. 1 (1991); *Smith v. Providence Health & Servs.-Oregon*, 361 Or. 456 (2017); *McKellips v. Saint Francis Hosp., Inc.*, 1987 OK 69 (1987); *Thompson v. Sun City Cmty. Hosp., Inc.*, 141 Ariz. 597 (1984); *Hastings v. Baton Rouge Gen. Hosp.*, 498 So. 2d 713 (La. 1986); Fangrow, *supra* note 3; Guest, *supra* note 3; and Charles Jones et al., *"The Loss of Chance" Doctrine in Medical Malpractice Cases*, Troutman Pepper (Mar. 13, 2013), www.troutman.com/insights/the-loss-of-chance-doctrine-in-medical-malpractice-cases.html.

vii. *See* Robert Solomon et al., *Cases and Materials on the Law of Torts* 1151 (Carswell 9th ed. 2015).

viii. *Id.* at 293.

ix. *Id.*; Dan B. Dobbs et al., *The Law of Torts § 125* (2d ed.), Westlaw (database updated July 2022).

x.   Solomon, *supra* note 8; Guest, *supra* note 3; Fangrow, *supra* note 3; Dobbs, *supra* note 9, at § 196; and [2005] UKHL 2.

xi. Solomon, *supra* note 8.

xii. *Id*.; Dobbs, *supra* note 9, at § 17.

xiii. Solomon, *supra* note 8.

xiv. *Id*.

xv. *Id*. at 294; Dobbs, *supra* note 12.

xvi. *Id*.

xvii. Solomon, *supra* note 8, at 294.

xviii. *Id*.; Dobbs, *supra* note 9, at § 121.

xix. Solomon, *supra* note 17; and *see also* Dobbs, *supra* note 9, at § 121.

xx. Solomon, *supra* note 17.

xxi. *Id*.; and Allan C. Hutchinson, *Some "What If" Thoughts: Notes on Donoghue v Stevenson*, 51 Osgoode Hall L. J. 706 (2014) (*"Donoghue* is an extension of a principle that Justice Benjamin Cardozo articulated in 1916 in the American case of *MacPherson v Buick Motor Co.*").

xxii. Solomon, *supra* note 17, at 295 and 304-8; and *Donoghue v. Stevenson*, [1932] AC 562, SC (HL) 31.

xxiii. Solomon, *supra* note 17, at 312.

xxiv. Franz Werro & Claudia Hasbun, *Is Macpherson A Legacy of Civilian Views?*, 9 J. Tort L. 67, 89 and 74 (2016) (*"MacPherson* explicitly influenced one of the most cited English decisions in tort law, *Donoghue v. Stevenson*").

xxv. 836 N.W.2d 321; 126 N.M. 807; 255 Kan. 199; 481 Pa. 256; 146 Haw. 540; 828 S.W.2d 681; 393 N.W.2d 131; 691 A.2d 641; 734 N.E.2d 535; 2003 WY 91; 107 Nev. 1 (1991); 361 Or. 456; 1987 OK 69; 141 Ariz. 597; 498 So. 2d 713; Solomon, *supra* note 17, at 297; Joanna Erdman et al., *Canadian Health Law and Policy* 307 (LexisNexis Canada, 5th ed. 2017); and *Saadati v. Moorhead*, 2017 SCC 28.

xxvi. Erdman, *supra* note 25, at 315; and Solomon, *supra* note 25, at 297.

xxvii. Erdman, *supra* note 25; Dobbs, *supra* note 9, at § 285; and Solomon, *supra* note 25, at 438.

xxviii. 452 Mass. at 12; Renehan, *supra* note 4; Joseph King, *Causation, Valuation, and Chance in Personal Injury Torts Involving Preexisting Conditions and Future Consequences*, 90 Yale L.J. 1353, 1356 (1981); and *Bigwood v. Bos.*, 209 Mass. 345, 348 (1911); Erdman et al., *supra* note 26; Ernest J. Weinrib, *Causal Uncertainty*, 36 Oxford J. Leg. Stud. 135 (2016); Vaughan Black, *The Rise and Fall of the Plaintiff-friendly Causation*, 53 Alta. L. Rev. 1014 (2016); Solomon, *supra* note 17, at 602-18; 836 N.W.2d at 344; Dobbs, *supra* note 9, at § 186 ("In a number of cases, however, the but-for test of factual cause puts the plaintiff out of court, even though the defendant is clearly negligent."); and Guest, *supra* note 3.

xxix. King, *supra* note 28, at 1355; Dobbs, *supra* note 9, at § 186; 2003 CanLII 50091; *Civil Liability Act 2002 No. 22* (NSW) § 5D; *Civil Liability Act 2002* (TAS) § 13; *Civil Liability Act 2003* (Qld) § 11; *Wrongs Act 1958* (VIC) § 51; *Civil Liability Act 1936* (SA) § 34; *Civil Law (Wrongs) Act 2002* (ACT) § 45; and *Civil Liability Act 2002* (WA) § 5C; Luntz, *supra* note 4, at 12; and Xiaowei Yu, *Causal Uncertainty in Chinese Medical Malpractice Law - When Theories Meet Facts*, 9 Tsinghua China L. Rev. 23, 33 (2016).

xxx. Erdman, *supra* note 26; Solomon, *supra* note 17, at 596; Nayha Acharya, *No More Chances for Lost Chances: A Weinribian Response to Weinrib*, 12 McGill J. L. & Health 205 (2019); and Dobbs, supra note 9, at § 186.

155

xxxi.   *Id.*

xxxii.   Renehan, *supra* note 4; Acharya, *supra* note 30, at 207-08; 452 Mass. at 12; King, *supra* note 28; Yu, *supra* note 29, at 31; and 209 Mass. at 348.

xxxiii. Renehan, *supra* note 4; 209 Mass. at 348; Acharya, *supra* note 32; 452 Mass. at 12; Yu, *supra* note 29, at 30-33; Luntz, *supra* note 4, at 25; and King, *supra* note 28.

xxxiv.   Solomon, *supra* note 17 at 602-18; *Snell v. Farrell*, 2 SCR 311 (1990); *Resurfice Corp. v. Hanke*, 1 SCR 333 (2007); *Clements v. Clements*, 2012 SCC 32; and Acharya, *supra* note 30, at 208-09.

xxxv.   Solomon, *supra* note 17 at 604; and 2 SCR 311.

xxxvi.   Solomon, *supra* note 35; 2 SCR 311; and Dobbs, *supra* note 9, at § 191 (showing that the same principle applies in the United States).

xxxvii. Solomon, *supra* note 35; 2 SCR 311; and *1653. Preponderance of Evidence*, West's ALR Digest Negligence k1653 (Nov. 2021 Update). Notably, there is no difference between the terms *balance of probabilities* and *preponderance of the evidence*. Both terms refer to equivalent standards, being *more likely than not* (51% or more). The United States utilizes the *preponderance* terminology, whereas Canada and the United Kingdom rely on the *balance of probabilities* phraseology. Comparably, Chinese law has adopted a much greater standard of proof, with some claiming it to be at least 70%. However, it being left to each judge's discretion, such high probability has not been utilized in practice, as members of the Chinese judiciary often employ or equate the Chinese standard of proof with the preponderance standard. *See* Yu, *supra* note 29, at 36 and n. 60.

xxxviii. Solomon, *supra* note 35; and Yu, *supra* note 29, at 28-29.

xxxix.   Solomon, *supra* note 35; Yu, *supra* note 29, at 34; and Luntz, *supra* note 33.

xl.   Solomon, *supra* note 35; Dobbs, *supra* note 9, at § 183; *Preponderance of Evidence*, *supra* note 37; Yu, *supra* note 39; *Civil Liability Act 2002 No. 22* (NSW) § 5E; *Civil Liability Act 2002* (TAS) § 14; *Civil Liability Act 2003* (Qld) § 12; *Wrongs Act 1958* (VIC) § 52; *Civil Liability Act 1936* (SA) § 35; *Civil Law (Wrongs) Act 2002* (ACT) § 46; *Civil Liability Act 2002* (WA) § 5D; and Luntz, *supra* note 33, at 27 ("The High Court of Australia refused to modify the requirement that the plaintiff in such an action must prove on the balance of probabilities that the defendant's negligence caused or contributed to the occurrence of the physical harm of which the plaintiff complains.").

xli.   2 SCR 311 (holding that causation may be inferred though no affirming nor scientific proof is provided); and Dobbs, *supra* note 9, at § 191.

xlii.   Solomon, *supra* note 35; and *TC by his tutor Sabatino v New South Wales & Ors*, [2001] NSWCA 380, para. 66 ("Questions of causation are not answered in a legal vacuum. Rather, they are answered in the legal framework in which they arise. For present purposes, that framework is the law of negligence.").

xliii.   Solomon, *supra* note 17 at 611; *Athey v. Leonati*, 3 SCR 458 (1996); and *Walker Estate v. York Finch General Hospital*, 2001 SCC 23.

xliv.   Solomon, *supra* note 43; 3 SCR 458; 2001 SCC 23; Black, *supra* note 28, at 1018 ("Presumably, the material contribution test was more plaintiff-favouring than the "but for" test, but beyond that *Athey* said nothing about what it meant and moreover nothing helpful about when this new (or at least new to Canada) alternative test might be available."); and for UK, *see Thorley v. Sandwell & West Birmingham Hospitals NHS Trust*, [2021] EWHC 2604 (QB), at para. 151

("Accordingly the claim of material contribution must fail on the basis that this modified test of causation does not apply when there is a single tortfeasor and an indivisible injury.").

xlv.   Solomon, *supra* note 17, at 611-12; and 1 SCR 333, at para. 25.

xlvi.   *Id.*

xlvii.   *Id.*

xlviii. 2012 SCC 32; Black, *supra* note 28, at 1018-19; and Samantha Galway & Gordon McKee, *Causation in Canada Revisited: Material Contribution to Risk and the Impact of Clements (Litigation Guardian of) v. Clements*, 83 Def. Couns. J. 487 (2016).

xlix.   2012 SCC 32, at para. 29; Black, *supra* note 28, at 1021; and Galway, *supra* note 48.

l.   2012 SCC 32 at para. 13 (limiting material contribution to "where it is impossible to determine which of a number of negligent acts by multiple actors in fact caused the injury, but it is established that one or more of them did in fact cause it."); Black, *supra* note 28, at 1022 and 1027; and Galway, *supra* note 48.

li.   1 2012 SCC 32 at para. 13 and 18 (referring to "the classic 'point the finger at someone else' defence": "the goals of tort law and the underlying theory of corrective justice require that the defendant not be permitted to escape liability by pointing the finger at another wrongdoer."); and Galway, *supra* note 48, at 490-91.

lii.   Galway, *supra* note 48, at 493-95; and Black, *supra* note 28, at 1027.

liii.   *Id.*

liv.   Galway, *supra* note 52; Black, *supra* note 52; *Dawes v. Gill*, 2019 ONSC 5649; and *Donleavy v. Ultramar Ltd.*, 2019 ONCA 687.

lv.   Civil Liability Act 2002 No 22 (NSW) § 5D; Civil Liability Act 2002 (TAS) § 13; Civil Liability Act 2003 (Qld) § 11 Wrongs Act 1958 (VIC) § 51; Civil Liability Act 1936 (SA) § 34; Civil Law (Wrongs) Act 2002 (ACT) § 45; Civil Liability Act 2002 (WA) § 5C; *Causation, Practical Law UK Glossary*, Westlaw UK (last visited Aug. 25, 2022); Mark Brookes et al., *The 'but for' test of causation in Australian law*, Carter Newell (Dec. 2020), https://www.carternewell.com/page/Publications/2020/the-but-for-test-of-causation-in-australian-law/ ("The various Civil Liability Acts confirm that factual causation requires the answering of the 'but for' causal question."); Galway, *supra* note 48, at 488; Black, *supra* note 52 ("[I]t is a "but for" world out there."); 2012 SCC 32, at para. 46 ("As a general rule, a plaintiff cannot succeed unless she shows as a matter of fact that she would not have suffered the loss "but for" the negligent act or acts of the defendant."); Acharya, *supra* note 30, at 207; and Peter M. Willcock & James M. Lepp, *Causation in Medical Negligence Cases*, at 1, The Canadian Bar Association (2008), http://www.cba.org/cba/cle/pdf/Causation in Medical Negligence Cases_paper.pdf.

lvi.   Dobbs, *supra* note 9, at § 191; 2 SCR 311; Black, *supra* note 28, at 1028; Erdman, *supra* note 26, at 316; Dympna Devenney, *In the absence of scientific certainty pointing towards a cause, the court must rely on the varying and contrasting professional opinions as to what occurred*, 27 M.L.J.I. 2021, at 96 (2021); *Briggs v. IAG Ltd. t/a NRMA Insur.*, [2022] NSWSC 372, at para. 70; *Seltsam Pty. Ltd. v. McGuiness*, [2000] NSWCA 29, at para. 143 ("An inference of causation for purposes of the tort of negligence may well be drawn when a scientist, including an epidemiologist, would not draw such an inference."); and *Metro North Hosp. and Health Service v. Pierce*, [2018] NSWCA 11, at para. 138 ("Whether the Hospital's negligence in not responding to the induced seizures in a timely manner materially contributed to Ms[.] Pierce's worsened condition is not to be determined on the basis of scientific certainty, but on the balance of probabilities.").

lvii. 2 SCR 311; Solomon, *supra* note 17, at 604-11; Black, *supra* note 28, at 1021; Dobbs, *supra* note 9, at § 183; Preponderance of Evidence, *supra* note 37; Civil Liability Act 2002 No. 22 (NSW) § 5E; Civil Liability Act 2002 (TAS) § 14; Civil Liability Act 2003 (Qld) § 12; Wrongs Act 1958 (VIC) § 52; Civil Liability Act 1936 (SA) § 35; Civil Law (Wrongs) Act 2002 (ACT) § 46; and Civil Liability Act 2002 (WA) § 5D.

lviii. 2 SCR 311; Solomon, *supra* note 17, at 611; and Restatement (Third) of Torts: Phys. & Emot. Harm § 3 (2010), Westlaw (database updated May 2022).

lix. 2 SCR 311; 2012 SCC 32; Erdman, *supra* note 56; Acharya, *supra* note 30, at 208; Black, *supra* note 28, at 1016; and [2001] NSWCA at para. 63.

lx. Stephanie Ben-Ishai & David R. Percy, *Contracts: Cases and Commentaries,* 822-24 (10th ed. Carswell 2018); and *Chaplin v. Hicks,* [1911] 2 K.B. 786.

lxi. *Id.*

lxii. *Id.*

lxiii. *Id.*

lxiv. *Id.*

lxv. *Id.*

lxvi. Renehan, *supra* note 4, at 14; 452 Mass. at 14; Black, *supra* note 28, at 1017 (stating that the loss of chance doctrine is greatly controversial in Canada and has been "comprehensively rejected in cases of medical negligence"); Luntz, *supra* note 4, at 6; Ben-Ishai *supra* note 60, at 824; *Gooding v. Univ. Hosp. Bldg., Inc.,* 445 So. 2d 1015, at 1019 (Fla. 1984); Acharya, *supra* note 30; and [2005] UKHL 2, at para. 226 ("The complexities of attempting to introduce liability for the loss of a chance of a more favourable outcome in personal injury claims have driven me, not without regret, to conclude that it should not be done.").

lxvii. *See* 2003 CanLII 50091; Luntz, *supra* note 4; King, *supra* note 28, at 1355; [2005] UKHL 2, at para. 15; and Dobbs, *supra* note 9, at § 186.

lxviii. 452 Mass. at 12; Renehan, *supra* note 4; 836 N.W.2d at 344; Luntz, *supra* note 4; and *see generally* Guest, *supra* note 3.

lxix. 2003 CanLII 50091; Luntz, *supra* note 4; and Guest, *supra* note 3.

lxx. *See e.g.,* Acharya, *supra* note 30; Weinrib, *supra* note 28, at 157-64; Luntz, *supra* note 4; Sonny Bal & Lawrence H. Brenner, *Medicolegal Sidebar: The Law and Social Values: Loss of Chance,* 472 Clin. Ortho. & Related Rsch. 2923 (2014); and Yu, *supra* note 29, at 45 ("Chinese courts are so flexible that they may apply either proportional liability or the lost chance doctrine to medical cases involving causal uncertainty at their discretion.").

lxxi. 2003 CanLII 50091; Acharya, *supra* note 30; Luntz, *supra* note 4; Erdman, *supra* note 26, at 315; and Solomon, *supra* note 17, at 618.

lxxii. [1991] 1 SCR 541.

lxxiii. *Id.*

lxxiv. *Id.*

lxxv. *Id.*

lxxvi. *Id.*

lxxvii.	*Id.*
lxxviii.	*Id.;* and Luntz, *supra* note 4.
lxxix.	*St-Jean v. Mercier*, [2002] 1 SCR 491; and Luntz, *supra* note 4.
lxxx.	*Id.*
lxxxi.	2003 CanLII 50091; and Luntz, *supra* note 4.
lxxxii.	*Id.*
lxxxiii.	*Id.*
lxxxiv.	*Id.*
lxxxv.	*Id.*
lxxxvi.	*Id.;* Acharya, *supra* note 30; Erdman, *supra* note 71; and Solomon, *supra* note 71.
lxxxvii.	*Hotson v. E. Berkshire Health Auth.*, [1987] 2 All ER 909; *Gregg v. Scott*, [2005] UKHL 2; and Luntz, *supra* note 4.
lxxxviii.	Luntz, *supra* note 4.
lxxxix.	*Id.;* and [1987] 2 All ER 909.
xc.	*Id.*
xci.	*Id.*
xcii.	[2005] UKHL 2; and Luntz, *supra* note 4.
xciii.	[2005] UKHL 2.
xciv.	*Id.*
xcv.	Luntz, *supra* note 4, at 27 ("With Tabet v Gett Australia has joined those common law jurisdictions which reject the doctrine of loss of chance in medical negligence cases.").
xcvi.	*Tabet v. Gett*, [2010] HCA 12, 240 CLR 537; and Luntz, *supra* note 4.
xcvii.	[2010] HCA 12.
xcviii.	*Id.*
xcix.	*Id.*
c.	*See, e.g.,* 452 Mass. 1; 836 N.W.2d 321; 126 N.M. 807; 255 Kan. at 218; 481 Pa. 256; 146 Haw. 540; 828 S.W.2d 681; 393 N.W.2d 131; 691 A.2d 641; 734 N.E.2d 535; 2003 WY 91; 107 Nev. 1; 361 Or. 456; 1987 OK 69; 141 Ariz. 597; 498 So. 2d 713; NH Rev. Stat. § 507-E:2 (2019); *Weymers v. Khera*, 454 Mich. 639, at 653 (1997); Mich. Comp. Laws Ann. § 600.2912a(2) (West); *Crosby v. United States*, 48 F.Supp.2d 924 (D. Alaska 1999); Alaska Stat. § 09.55.540; and *Kemper v. Gordon*, 272 S.W.3d 146, 159 (Ky. 2008).
ci.	Guest, *supra* note 3; and Luntz, *supra* note 4.
cii.	*See, e.g.,* 452 Mass. 1; 836 N.W.2d 321; 126 N.M. 807; 255 Kan. at 218; 481 Pa. 256; 146 Haw. 540; 828 S.W.2d 681; 393 N.W.2d 131; 691 A.2d 641; 734 N.E.2d 535; 2003 WY 91; 107 Nev. 1; 361 Or. 456; 1987 OK 69; 141 Ariz. 597; and 498 So. 2d 713.
ciii.	452 Mass. at 26-28; Renehan, *supra* note 38, at 14; and 836 N.W.2d at 335.
civ.	452 Mass. at 5.
cv.	*Id.*
cvi.	*Id.* at 10-11.
cvii.	*Id.*
cviii.	*Id.* at 30.
cix.	*Id.*
cx.	*Id.* at 27.

cxi.   *Id.*

cxii.   *Id.*

cxiii.   452 Mass. at 26-27 ("The most widely adopted of these methods of valuation is the 'proportional damages' approach."); 836 N.W.2d at 335; and 734 N.E.2d at 541.

cxiv.   Guest, *supra* note 3; Fangrow, *supra* note 3; and *see also* Jones, *supra* note 6.

cxv.   Tory A. Weigand, *Lost Chances, Felt Necessities, and the Tale of Two Cities*, 43 Suffolk U.L. Rev. 327, 327-28 and 381-82 (2010) ("The Kemper and Matsuyama decisions capture the debate over whether medical malpractice liability should be expanded to include responsibility for lost chances of a better outcome, as well as the divergent views as to the appropriate role and limits to judicial power and policymaking as to physician liability.").

cxvi.   *Kemper v. Gordon*, 272 S.W.3d 146, 148 (Ky. 2008).

cxvii.   *Id.*

cxviii.   *Id.*

cxix.   *Id.*

cxx.   *Id.*

cxxi.   *Id.*

cxxii.   272 S.W.3d at 149.

cxxiii.   *Id.*

cxxiv.   *Id.*

cxxv.   *Id.*

cxxvi.   272 S.W.3d at 146.

cxxvii.   272 S.W.3d at 148.

cxxviii. 272 S.W.3d at 152 ("We are troubled by the potential financial burden that might be spread upon the shoulders of millions of people if we adopt this new concept of lost or diminished chance of recovery.").

cxxix.   272 S.W.3d at 152-53 (citing *Smith v. Parrott*, 2003 VT 64, 175 Vt. 375, 833 A.2d 843, 848 (2003)).

cxxx.   Guest, *supra* note 3; Fangrow, *supra* note 3; and *see also* Jones, *supra* note 6; 452 Mass. 1; 836 N.W.2d 321; 126 N.M. 807; 255 Kan. at 218; 481 Pa. 256; 146 Haw. 540; 828 S.W.2d 681; 393 N.W.2d 131; 691 A.2d 641; 734 N.E.2d 535; 2003 WY 91; 107 Nev. 1; 361 Or. 456; 1987 OK 69; 141 Ariz. 597; 498 So. 2d 713; NH Rev. Stat. § 507-E:2 (2019); 454 Mich. 639, at 653 (1997); Mich. Comp. Laws Ann. § 600.2912a(2) (West); 48 F.Supp.2d 924 (D. Alaska 1999); Alaska Stat. § 09.55.540; and 272 S.W.3d 146, 159 (Ky. 2008).

cxxxi.   452 Mass. at 26-28; and 272 S.W.3d at 161.

cxxxii.   *See* Gould, *supra* note 1.

cxxxiii. 452 Mass. at 27.

cxxxiv.   452 Mass. at 26-27; 836 N.W.2d at 335; and 734 N.E.2d at 541

cxxxv.   452 Mass. at 26 ("The most widely adopted of these methods of valuation is the 'proportional damages' approach."); 836 N.W.2d at 335; and *Cahoon v. Cummings*, 734 N.E.2d 535, 541 (Ind. 2000).

cxxxvi.   272 S.W.3d at 161.

cxxxvii. 272 S.W.3d at 159.

cxxxviii. 452 Mass. at 26-28; and 272 S.W.3d at 161.

cxxxix.   *See* Gould, *supra* note 1. One might argue there are other factors of relevance beyond for instance those considered in staging based on TNM. *See* 452 Mass. at 8–9, stating:

    a.   Finkel offered an extensive discussion of the tumor-lymph nodes-metastasis (TNM) method for classifying gastric cancer into separate "stages,".... Patients with stage 0, in which the cancer is confined to the stomach lining, have a better than 90% survival rate, Finkel averred; at stage 1, the survival rate drops to between 60% and 80%; at stage 2, between 30% and 50%; at stage 3, between 10% and 20%; and at stage 4, less than 4%.17 Finkel opined that, as a result of Birnbaum's breach of the standard of care, Matsuyama lost the opportunity of having gastric cancer "diagnosed and treated in a timely fashion when it might still have been curable."

cxl.   272 S.W.3d at 161.

cxli.   *Id.*

cxlii.   *See e.g.*, 836 N.W.2d at 349 n. 14.

cxliii.   Acharya, *supra* note 30, at 207.

cxliv.   Weinrib, *supra* note 28, at 139.

cxlv.   *Id.* at 157.

cxlvi.   *Id.*

cxlvii.   *Id.*

cxlviii.   *Id.*

cxlix.   *Id.* at 158.

cl.   *Id.*

cli.   *Id.*

clii.   *Id.*

cliii.   *Id.*

cliv.   *Id.* at 160.

clv.   *Id.*

clvi.   *Id.*

clvii.   *Id.* at 161-63.

clviii.   *Id.*

clix.   *Id.*

clx.   *Id.* at 163.

clxi.   *Id.*

clxii.   *Id.*

clxiii.   Acharya, *supra* note 30, at 221-24.

clxiv.   *Id.* at 223.

clxv.   *Id.* at 222-23.

clxvi.   *Id.* at 223.

clxvii.   *Id.* ("In the same way, accommodating factual uncertainty by resorting to the loss of chance doctrine may appear desirable because it would afford an injured individual some compensation, but such piecemeal justification is inappropriate.").

clxviii.   *Id.*

clxix.   *Id.* at 214.

clxx.   *Id.*

clxxi.   *Id.* at 218-19.

clxxii.   *Id.*

clxxiii.   *Id.* at 219 ("Suppose…a patient is sent to a specialist for a chest x-ray. That specialist negligently misreads the x-ray and assures the patient's physician that she has a benign condition that requires no treatment. As a result of the misdiagnosis, the specialist has in fact not undertaken to improve the chances of survival at all.").

clxxiv.   *See* Consent to Treatment, College of Physicians and Surgeons of Ontario (2001), http://www.cpso.on.ca/Physicians/Policies-Guidance/Policies/Consent-to-Treatment - Endnotes; and Health Care Consent Act, SO 1996, c. 2.

clxxv.   *Coody v. Barraza*, 111 So. 3d 485 (2013) (holding that jury was correct in finding that defendant-radiologist's failure to abide by the requisite standard resulted in Ms. Coody suffering a loss of a chance, with respect to her survival or obtaining a better outcome).

clxxvi.   Acharya, *supra* note 30, at 220.

clxxvii.   *Id.* at 224-25.

clxxviii. *Id.* at 205-25.

clxxix.   *Kemp v. Balboa*, 959 S.W.2d 116 (Mo. Ct. App. 1997), *opinion adopted and reinstated after retransfer* (Mar. 2, 1998); and *Wollen v. DePaul Health Ctr.*, 828 S.W.2d 681 (Mo. 1992).

clxxx.   959 S.W.2d at 119 ("We are unable to conclude that Wollen opened the door to "lost chance of recovery" claims in every tort action in which a plaintiff contends that his physical injuries may have shortened his life…action was not a medical malpractice action."); and Steven R. Koch, *Whose Loss Is It Anyway? Effects of the "Lost-Chance" Doctrine on Civil Litigation and Medical Malpractice Insurance*, 88 N.C. L. Rev. 595, 631-32 (2010).

clxxxi.   Koch, *supra* note 167.

clxxxii.   *See e.g., Fennell v. S. Maryland Hosp. Ctr., Inc.*, 320 Md. 776, 797, 580 A.2d 206, 217 (1990) ("the majority should not be so quick to adopt the parade of horribles so facilely conjured up by the defense bar. It is not inevitable that "societal costs" (i.e. insurance premiums) would be increased should this approach to damages be applied, or that new floodgates of litigation will open.").

clxxxiii. *See e.g.*, 272 S.W.3d at 152 and 161 ("A whole new and expensive industry of experts could conceivably be marched through our courts, providing evidence for juries that an MRI misread on Monday, but accurately discerned on Friday, perhaps gives rise to an infinitesimal loss of a chance to recover. Yet, under this doctrine, even a small percentage of the value of a human life could generate substantial recovery and place burdensome costs on healthcare providers. This additional financial load would be passed along to every man, woman, and child in this Commonwealth.").

clxxxiv.   Steven R. Koch, *Whose Loss Is It Anyway? Effects of the "Lost-Chance" Doctrine on Civil Litigation and Medical Malpractice Insurance*, 88 N.C. L. Rev. 595, at 619-27 (2010) ("While the volatility of claims paid per year is substantial, an analysis of malpractice insurance premium payments in several states that addressed the lost-chance doctrine in the mid-1990s indicates that the economic effect of such an adoption can be nothing more than a proverbial drop in the bucket.").

clxxxv.   House of Commons, *NHS litigation reform*, UK Parliament (2022), https://committees.parliament.uk/publications/22039/documents/163739/default/ (last visited Sep. 7, 2022) ("At the same time, the costs of the system have continued to grow at an eye-watering rate… This sum is set to double over the next decade to £4.6 billion, and around a quarter of such costs go not to families but to lawyers. The English NHS spends 2% of its total income on clinical negligence compared to half that level in New Zealand or Sweden.").

clxxxvi. 272 S.W.3d at 152 ("We are troubled by the potential financial burden that might be spread upon the shoulders of millions of people if we adopt this new concept of lost or diminished chance of recovery.").

clxxxvii. Koch, *supra* note 167, at 626-30 ("various factors other than medical malpractice claims themselves appear to be the driving force behind the malpractice insurance premium rates… a particular state's adoption of the lost-chance doctrine is even more tangentially related to any potential effect that medical malpractice claims may have on malpractice insurance rates. . . .").

clxxxviii. Tory A. Weigand, Esq., *Lost Chances, Felt Necessities, and the Tale of Two Cities*, 43 Suffolk U. L. Rev. 327, 374 (2010); and *see also Fennell v. S. Maryland Hosp. Ctr., Inc.*, 320 Md. 776, 789–90, 580 A.2d 206, 213 (1990).

clxxxix. 320 Md. at 789–90, 580 A.2d at 213 (1990).

cxc. 452 Mass. at 29 ("As we have noted, probabilistic evidence, in the form of actuarial tables, assumptions about present value and future interest rates, statistical measures of future harm, and the like, is the stock-in-trade of tort valuation.").

cxci. 452 Mass. at 29 ("For decades, judges, lawyers, jurors, and litigants have shown themselves competent to sift through such evidence in a variety of contexts, from mass toxic torts to single-car collisions.").

cxcii. *Fennell v. S. Maryland Hosp. Ctr., Inc.*, 320 Md. 776, 789–90, 580 A.2d 206, 213 (1990)

cxciii. Tory A. Weigand, *Lost Chances, Felt Necessities, and the Tale of Two Cities*, 43 Suffolk U. L. Rev. 327, 374 (2010).

cxciv. *Id.* at 366 (*citing* Robert Kaplan, *Disease, Diagnosis, & Dollars* 4 & 35 (2009)).

cxcv. *Id.* at 366.

cxcvi. *Id.* at 365-70.

cxcvii. *See e.g.*, 836 N.W.2d 321; 126 N.M. 807; 255 Kan. 199; 481 Pa. 256; 146 Haw. 540; 828 S.W.2d 681; 393 N.W.2d 131; 691 A.2d 641; 734 N.E.2d 535; 2003 WY 91, *on reh'g* 2004 WY 44; 107 Nev. 1 (1991); 361 Or. 456; 1987 OK 69; 141 Ariz. 597; 498 So. 2d 713; 452 Mass. 1; 454 Mich. 639; 48 F.Supp.2d 924; and 272 S.W.3d 146.

cxcviii. *Kemper v. Gordon*, 272 S.W.3d 146, 148-49 (Ky. 2008).

cxcix. *Gordon v. Kemper*, No. 2002-CA-001983-MR, Cross-Appeal No. 2002-CA-002043-MR, (Ky. Ct. App. Mar. 25, 2005) ("Lori believed that something was physically wrong with her. Lori was so fatigued that she could barely get out of bed and so nauseated that she could hardly eat. She reported hair loss, chronic urinary tract infections, and severe chest pains.").

cc. Tory Weigand, Lost Chances, Felt Necessities, and the Tale of Two Cities, 43 Suffolk U. L. Rev. 327, 373 (2010) ("Additionally, imposing liability upon physicians for any statistical loss of a better outcome can only fuel defensive medicine.").

cci. *Id.* at 342–43 (2010).

ccii. *Id.* at 343.

cciii. Koch, *supra* note 167, at 626-30 ("various factors other than medical malpractice claims themselves appear to be the driving force behind the malpractice insurance premium rates… a particular state's adoption of the lost-chance doctrine is even more tangentially related to any potential effect that medical malpractice claims may have on malpractice insurance rates. . . .").

cciv.   Tory A. Weigand, *Lost Chances, Felt Necessities, and the Tale of Two Cities*, 43 Suffolk U. L. Rev. 327, 342–43 (2010).

ccv.   Eddie Harmon-Jones & Judson Mills, *An Introduction to Cognitive Dissonance Theory and an Overview of Current Perspectives on the Theory, in Cognitive dissonance: Reexamining a pivotal theory in psychology* (2nd ed.) 3–24, at 3 (Eddie Harmon-Jones ed., 2019), http://content.apa.org/books/16109-001.

ccvi.   Shawn Eyer, *Translation from Plato's Republic 514b–518d* ("*Allegory of the Cave*"), Harvard Uni. Pub. (2009), https://scholar.harvard.edu/files/seyer/files/plato_republic_514b-518d_allegory-of-the-cave.pdf; and *see also Plato's Allegory of the Cave Explained*, MasterClass (Nov. 2021 Update), https://www.masterclass.com/articles/allegory-of-the-cave-explained.

ccvii.   *Id.*

ccviii.   *Id.*

ccix.   *Id.*

ccx.   *Id.*

ccxi.   *Id.*

ccxii.   *Id.*

ccxiii.   Eddie Harmon-Jones & Judson Mills, *An Introduction to Cognitive Dissonance Theory and an Overview of Current Perspectives on the Theory, in Cognitive dissonance: Reexamining a pivotal theory in psychology* (2nd ed.) 3–24 (Eddie Harmon-Jones ed., 2019), http://content.apa.org/books/16109-001.

ccxiv.   *Id.*

ccxv.   *Id.* at 4.

ccxvi.   *See* Michael Flynn, *The Unwritten Rules of Sports and Medical Malpractice*, 19 J. Health Care L. & Pol'y 73, 77 (2017):

    a.   The "conspiracy of silence" among doctors embodies the notion that testifying against a fellow doctor in a medical malpractice case is akin to betrayal and is grounds for punishment. This "conspiracy of silence" has led to an implicit reluctance from members of the medical community to testify on behalf of plaintiffs and has established an unwritten rule among medical professionals of not testifying against your fellow doctor. Anyone who breaks this rule is dubbed a traitor and publicly labeled a "hired gun," embodying the idea that expert witnesses are for sale and that attorneys can actively shop for those willing to support their cause. In fact, the problem has become so widespread that the "so-called conspiracy of silence has been recognized as a matter of judicial notice [across the country]."

ccxvii.   *Armstrong v. Royal Victoria Hospital*, 2019 ONCA 963; and *Armstrong v. Ward*, 2021 SCC 1.

ccxviii.   2019 ONCA 963, at para. 106.

ccxix.   2019 ONCA 963, at paras. 107-10.

ccxx.   2019 ONCA 963, at paras. 107-10.

ccxxi.   2019 ONCA 963, at paras. 109.

ccxxii.   2019 ONCA 963, at paras. 109 ("Dr. Hagen confirmed that it was necessary for the surgeon to stay two millimetres away from the ureter and that if the surgeon had properly identified and protected the ureter "you wouldn't have this injury". However he refused to admit that Dr. Ward might have failed to do so, or if he did that he would have breached the standard of care…").

ccxxiii. Katie Serena, *Meet Ted Bundy's Mom, Eleanor Louise Cowell, Who Never Questioned His Innocence*, ati (2019), https://allthatsinteresting.com/eleanor-louise-cowell.

ccxxiv. *Id.*

ccxxv. Eddie Harmon-Jones & Judson Mills, *An Introduction to Cognitive Dissonance Theory and an Overview of Current Perspectives on the Theory, in Cognitive dissonance: Reexamining a pivotal theory in psychology* (2nd ed.) 3–24, at 4 (Eddie Harmon-Jones ed., 2019), http://content.apa.org/books/16109-001.

ccxxvi. Yet another example of cognitive dissonance can be found in the following fictional scenario: Chris, a 12-year-old with a proclivity for luxury items and fast-food, has a parent, Mrs. Kroc, who believes her child can do no wrong. In fact, over the years, Mrs. Kroc has spoiled Chris to no end, resulting in him being ill-disciplined, entitled, and egocentrically-regressed. Well, Chris ended up getting into a fist-fight with *Randy*, another student at school, and was subsequently brought to the principal's office. Despite this, no punishment ever was handed down to Chris. Instead, blame fell upon Randy, an individual who was dwarfed in size by Chris. Why you ask? Chris showed his mother text messages from Randy that suggested Randy was bullying Chris, and in fact, was the one who initiated the fight. Armed with this information, Mrs. Kroc had the principal suspend Randy and issue a formal apology to Chris. The one problem is, the text messages Chris showed to his mother were completely fabricated by Chris and his friend Bob. When Randy finds out, he tells Mrs. Kroc and the Principal, and even goes so far as to show them both how the text messages were faked, but Mrs. Kroc refuses to believe that her son would do such a thing, after all, she exclaims, "Chris is the most honest boy in the world." Why do you think Mrs. Kroc would refuse to believe, or even question her son, in the face of such new information?

ccxxvii. Tory A. Weigand, *Lost Chances, Felt Necessities, and the Tale of Two Cities*, 43 Suffolk U. L. Rev. 327, 373 (2010) ("[a]dditionally, imposing liability upon physicians for any statistical loss of a better outcome can only fuel defensive medicine.").

ccxxviii. *Id.* at 373.

ccxxix. 272 S.W.3d at 161 ("Lost chance is never reached by the trier of fact unless it also finds that a physician acted negligently toward his or her patient.").

ccxxx. Tory A. Weigand, *Lost Chances, Felt Necessities, and the Tale of Two Cities*, 43 Suffolk U. L. Rev. 327, 373 (2010); and 272 S.W.3d at 152 ("Yet, under this doctrine, even a small percentage of the value of a human life could generate substantial recovery and place burdensome costs on healthcare providers.").

ccxxxi. Tory A. Weigand, *Lost Chances, Felt Necessities, and the Tale of Two Cities*, 43 Suffolk U. L. Rev. 327, 373 (2010) ("Moreover, if statistical chances, no matter how small, are the basis for liability, why wouldn't healthcare providers simply order any and all testing and procedure regardless of efficacy?").

ccxxxii. *Id.* at 373.

ccxxxiii. 272 S.W.3d at 147–52 ("We are troubled by the potential financial burden that might be spread upon the shoulders of millions of people if we adopt this new concept of lost or diminished chance of recovery.").

ccxxxiv. 272 S.W.3d at 148–50.

ccxxxv.   452 Mass. at 26 ("The most widely adopted of these methods of valuation is the 'proportional damages' approach."); 836 N.W.2d at 335; and *Cahoon v. Cummings*, 734 N.E.2d 535, 541 (Ind. 2000).

ccxxxvi.   272 S.W.3d at 159 (Noble, J., dissenting).

ccxxxvii.   452 Mass. at 26; 836 N.W.2d at 335; and 734 N.E.2d at 541.

ccxxxviii. 452 Mass. at 26; 836 N.W.2d at 335; and 734 N.E.2d at 541.

ccxxxix.   272 S.W.3d at 159 (Noble, J., dissenting).

ccxl.   *Percentage Change and Percentage Point Change: A Primer*, www.reed.edu (2010), https://www.reed.edu/percent (last visited Apr. 15, 2022); and Alvan R. Feinstein, *Invidious Comparisons and Unmet Clinical Challenges*, 92 AM. J. Med. 117 (1992).

ccxli.   *See* Gould, *supra* note 1 (breaking down and showing usefulness of survival distribution).

ccxlii.   Alvan R. Feinstein, *Invidious Comparisons and Unmet Clinical Challenges*, 92 AM. J. Med. 117 (1992); Cf. Lars Noah, *An Inventory of Mathematical Blunders in Applying the Loss-of-A-Chance Doctrine*, 24 Rev. Litig. 369, 394 (2005) (presenting the attributable risk calculation); and Zaven T. Saroyan, *The Current Injustice of the Loss of Chance Doctrine: An Argument for A New Approach to Damages*, 33 Cumb. L. Rev. 15, 36 (2003) (presenting the Relative Proportionality Approach: (.5) x [(the proportion of loss) x (the remaining value of the injured person's life)]). Notably, the Walker Approach to calculating damages was completely created independently from Zaven Saroyan's Relative Proportionality Approach and that of the attributable risk calculation, or approaches that may be deemed similar in any respect (*Feist Publications, Inc. v. Rural Tel. Serv. Co.*, 499 U.S. 340 (1991); 17 U.S.C.A. § 101 (West)); U.S. Const. art. I, § 8, cl. 8). Access and review of these approaches was only obtained years later after the Walker Approach had been formulated. Having since reviewed these approaches, a discussion will follow that distinguishes the Walker Approach from them.

ccxliii.   What would be the result if we apply this scenario to the variants detailed in Exercise: A Relative Analysis in Place of a Threshold One? **Under the first variant**, i.e., *the traditional approach +*, Mr. Wick again recovers full damages, however, Mr. Baggins recovers $20,000. **Under the second variant**, *i.e., pro rata extremus*, Mr. Wick recovers $10,000, and Mr. Baggins recovers $20,000. How do you feel about these results?

ccxliv.   *See e.g.*, 2003 CanLII 50091; 836 N.W.2d 321; 126 N.M. 807; 255 Kan. 199; 481 Pa. 256; 146 Haw. 540; 828 S.W.2d 681; 393 N.W.2d 131; 691 A.2d 641; 734 N.E.2d 535; 2003 WY 91, *on reh'g* 2004 WY 44; 107 Nev. 1 (1991); 361 Or. 456; 1987 OK 69; 141 Ariz. 597; 498 So. 2d 713; 452 Mass. 1; 454 Mich. 639; 48 F.Supp.2d 924; and 272 S.W.3d 146.

ccxlv.   272 S.W.3d at 159 (Noble, J., dissenting).

ccxlvi.   *Id.* at 161 ("While not physical, the loss of the chance for a better recovery is real, and it resonates with anyone who has ever been denied an opportunity for something important.").

ccxlvii.   *Id.* ("plaintiff need only show a better than 50% chance in order to recover the full measure of damages against the physician.").

ccxlviii.   *See e.g.*, 580 A.2d at 209 ("For example, if the patient had a 40% chance of recovery and negligent treatment reduced the patient's chance of survival to 10%, then the actual loss of chance of survival would be 30%."); and 741 P.2d at 477 ("To illustrate the method in a case where the jury determines from the statistical findings combined with the specific facts relevant to the patient the patient originally had a 40% chance of cure and the physician's negligence

	reduced the chance of cure to 25%, (40% − 25%) 15% represents the patient's loss of survival. If the total amount of damages proved by the evidence is $500,000, the damages caused by defendant is 15% x $500,000 or $75,000.").
ccxlix.	Alvan R. Feinstein, *Invidious Comparisons and Unmet Clinical Challenges*, 92 AM. J. Med. 117 (1992); *Cf.* Lars Noah, *An Inventory of Mathematical Blunders in Applying the Loss-of-A-Chance Doctrine*, 24 Rev. Litig. 369, 394 (2005) (presenting the attributable risk calculation); and Zaven T. Saroyan, *The Current Injustice of the Loss of Chance Doctrine: An Argument for A New Approach to Damages*, 33 Cumb. L. Rev. 15, 36 (2003) (presenting the Relative Proportionality Approach: (.5) x [(the proportion of loss) x (the remaining value of the injured person's life)]). Notably, the Walker Approach to calculating damages was completely created independently from Zaven Saroyan's Relative Proportionality Approach and that of the attributable risk calculation, or approaches that may be deemed similar in any respect (*Feist Publications, Inc. v. Rural Tel. Serv. Co.*, 499 U.S. 340 (1991); 17 U.S.C.A. § 101 (West)); U.S. Const. art. I, § 8, cl. 8). Access and review of these approaches was only obtained years later after the Walker Approach had been formulated. Having since reviewed these approaches, a discussion will follow that distinguishes the Walker Approach from them.
ccl.	*Herskovits v. Grp. Health Co-op. of Puget Sound*, 99 Wash. 2d 609, 614 and 619, 664 P.2d 474, 476 and 479 (1983) ("such negligence was the proximate cause of reducing his chances of survival by 14 percent."). Appreciably, even though Justice Dore recognizes that the reduction from 39% to 25% equates to a 36% reduction in the patient's chance of survival, he no less references the loss as 14% throughout the majority opinion. *Id.* at 614 and 610-19. *In fact,* the 14% figure is referenced 8 times throughout the opinion, whereas 36% is referenced only once. *Id.* at 610-45.
ccli.	*Herskovits v. Grp. Health Co-op. of Puget Sound*, 99 Wash. 2d 609, 622, 664 P.2d 474, 480 (1983) (Pearson, J., *concurring*) ("Therefore, the only indications from the record of the extent of the reduction in Mr. Herskovits' chance of long-term survival are that it was "substantial" and that it was at most a 14 percent reduction (from 39 percent to 25 percent)").
cclii.	Patricia L. Andel, *Comment, Medical Malpractice: The Right to Recover for the Loss of a Chance of Survival*, 12 Pepp. L. Rev. 973, 995 n.104 (1985) ("Referring to the decedent's reduction in chance from 39% to 25%, the court properly recognized that this was a 36% reduction in the decedent's chance of survival, rather than making the common mistake of calculating this reduction as a 14% decrease (as did the medical expert in his testimony), which relates to the physician's degree of causation of the actual death"). According to Lars Noah, Patricia "then immediately failed to apply her own preferred method of calculation. *See id.* at 996-97 (discussing a hypothetical loss of a 40% chance of survival)." Lars Noah, *An Inventory of Mathematical Blunders in Applying the Loss-of-A-Chance Doctrine*, 24 Rev. Litig. 369, 405 n. 20 (2005). However, upon further review of the footnotes, it appears arguably that one of two things is occurring: (1) that Lars is incorrect, as Patricia does in fact state that she is using the method of the equation in n.104, and therefore, Patricia incorrectly applies that equation, arriving at 40%, when she ought to have reached 100% instead; or (2) Patricia mixes apples with oranges, failing to appreciate that the method for computing percent difference is different from percentage probability, as in applying the latter, Patricia arrived at 40%, when she would have reached 100% had she calculated percent difference. Patricia L. Andel, *Comment, Medical*

	Malpractice: The Right to Recover for the Loss of a Chance of Survival, 12 Pepp. L. Rev. 973, at 995-97 and n.110 (1985). Ultimately, one thing that is clear is that Patricia incorrectly offers the formula utilized to calculate percent difference as an example of an equation using the method in the percentage probability test. *Id*. at 996 n.110.
ccliii.	Zaven Saroyan, *The Current Injustice of the Loss of Chance Doctrine: An Argument for A New Approach to Damages*, 33 Cumb. L. Rev. 15 (2003).
ccliv.	Zaven Saroyan, *The Current Injustice of the Loss of Chance Doctrine: An Argument for A New Approach to Damages*, 33 Cumb. L. Rev. 15, 36 (2003).
cclv.	Aside from simply attempting to approximate "the multiplier method previously and consistently used by the courts," no other justification as to why loss of chance recovery ought to be cut in half is seemingly afforded. *Id*. at 37-8.
cclvi.	*Id*. at 38 ("This calculation includes the use of mortality tables (intended to find the average life expectancy of an individual given differing variables) combined with the amount of income that individual would have earned given their present income and often their prospects for advancement.").
cclvii.	*Id*. at 42 n. 189.
cclviii.	*Id*. at 42 n. 189.
cclix.	*Id*. at 42 n. 189.
cclx.	*Id*. at 42 n. 189.
cclxi.	It appears as though Saroyan recognizes the flaws of his approach, stating "The method of valuation the author proposes, though admitting its inherent flaws, comes closer to something that is more...." *Id*. at 40.
cclxii.	*Id*. at 42 n. 189.
cclxiii.	Lars Noah, *An Inventory of Mathematical Blunders in Applying the Loss-of-A-Chance Doctrine*, 24 Rev. Litig. 369, 378 (2005).
cclxiv.	*See e.g.*, Melissa M. Thompson, *Causal Inference in Epidemiology: Implications for Toxic Tort Litigation*, 71 N.C. L. Rev. 247 (1992) (applying attributable risk in the context of toxic tort litigation); and Vern R. Walker, *Direct Interference in the Lost Chance Cases: Factfinding Constraints Under Minimal Fairness to Parties*, 23 Hofstra L. Rev. 247, 307 n. 14 (1994) ("Thus, a point estimate of the relative risk of death from being in the reference situation (with defendant's negligence), as compared to the risk from being in the reference situation but absent the defendant's negligence, is 75 /61 = 1.23.").
cclxv.	Lars Noah, *An Inventory of Mathematical Blunders in Applying the Loss-of-A-Chance Doctrine*, 24 Rev. Litig. 369, 394 (2005).
cclxvi.	*Id*.
cclxvii.	*Id*. at 395 ("Instead of asking about the loss of a chance for survival, courts should focus on the flip-side question framed as the increased risk of morbidity and mortality.").
cclxviii.	*Id*. at 394.
cclxix.	*Id*.
cclxx.	*Id*.
cclxxi.	*Id*.
cclxxii.	*Id*.

cclxxiii. Lars Noah, *An Inventory of Mathematical Blunders in Applying the Loss-of-A-Chance Doctrine*, 24 Rev. Litig. 369, 394 (2005).

cclxxiv. *Id.* at 398-99.

cclxxv. *Id.*

cclxxvi. *Id.* at 399.

cclxxvii. Lars Noah, *An Inventory of Mathematical Blunders in Applying the Loss-of-A-Chance Doctrine*, 24 Rev. Litig. 369, 399–400 (2005).

cclxxviii. 272 S.W.3d at 161 (Noble, J., dissenting) ("plaintiff need only show a better than 50% chance in order to recover the full measure of damages against the physician.").

cclxxix. Lars Noah, *An Inventory of Mathematical Blunders in Applying the Loss-of-A-Chance Doctrine*, 24 Rev. Litig. 369, 399 (2005).

cclxxx. Lars Noah, *An Inventory of Mathematical Blunders in Applying the Loss-of-A-Chance Doctrine*, 24 Rev. Litig. 369, 398–99 (2005).

cclxxxi. *Note*: It is assumed that the *patient-plaintiff* would receive 66.7% of the damages, rather than full damages, as Noah states in the preceding paragraph he would award 80% of the damages. *Id.* at 399.

cclxxxii. *See* 272 S.W.3d at 161 (Noble, J., dissenting) ("plaintiff need only show a better than 50% chance in order to recover the full measure of damages against the physician.").

cclxxxiii. Noah, *supra* note 279.

cclxxxiv. *Id.* at 402-03.

cclxxxv. *Id.*

cclxxxvi. *Id.*

cclxxxvii. *Id.*

cclxxxviii. Lars Noah, *An Inventory of Mathematical Blunders in Applying the Loss-of-A-Chance Doctrine*, 24 Rev. Litig. 369, 394–97 and 404 (2005).

cclxxxix. *Id.*

ccxc. See 272 S.W.3d at 161 (Noble, J., dissenting) ("Every patient in this scenario doubtless feels that a tangible thing has been lost when they are denied their chance for a better result.").

ccxci. *Id.* ("While not physical, the loss of the chance for a better recovery is real, and it resonates with anyone who has ever been denied an opportunity for something important.").

ccxcii. Melissa M. Thompson, *Causal Inference in Epidemiology: Implications for Toxic Tort Litigation*, 71 N.C. L. Rev. 247, 252 n.32 (1992).

ccxciii. Robert Goff, *Tantalizing Tantalus*, Forbes (Feb. 23, 1998) https://www.forbes.com/forbes/1998/0223/6104154a.html?sh=db747d1306c7.

ccxciv. *Reibl v. Hughes*, [1980] 2 SCR 880.

ccxcv. Andrew M. Palmer, *Kemper v. Gordon: The Kentucky Supreme Court Forecloses the Loss-of-Chance Doctrine in Medical-Malpractice Cases*, 48 U. Louisville L. Rev. 639 (2010) (Notably, these "rational" answers are comparable to those proffered by students of Professor David Leibson, upon his presenting of a similar scenario).

ccxcvi. Analysis informed and based on that presented by amspencer1984, *Quote of the week: The Opposite of a Profound Truth, Niels Bohr*, LifeThinkBlog (March 8, 2013), https://lifethinkblog.wordpress.com/2013/03/08/quote-of-the-week-the-opposite-of-a-profound-truth-niels-bohr/.

ccxcvii. *What Is Nanotechnology?* Nat'l Nanotech. Initiative, https://www.nano.gov/nanotech-101/what/definition (last visited Apr. 12, 2022) ("One nanometer is a billionth of a meter, or 10-9 of a meter.").

ccxcviii. *See* Matthew Calloway Walker, *Nano-Bots, Doctors in Disguise: Exploring Loss of Chance at the Nano-Level* (2022); and *Id.*

ccxcix. Tobias Esch & George B. Stefano, *The Neurobiology of Love*, Neuro Endocrinol Lett. 2005 Jun;26(3):175-92. PMID: 15990719.

ccc. Jerry Maguire (1996); The Princess Bride (1987); The Empire Strikes Back (1980); and Harry Potter and the Deathly Hallows: Part II (2011).

ccci. *The Aesop for Children*, Library of Congress, *adapted from The Aesop for Children: with Pictures by Milo Winter*, (Rand, McNally & Co. 1919), https://read.gov/aesop/114.html.

cccii. *See e.g.*, Andrew M. Palmer, *Kemper v. Gordon: The Kentucky Supreme Court Forecloses the Loss-of-Chance Doctrine in Medical-Malpractice Cases*, 48 U. Louisville L. Rev. 646-652 (2010) (Analyzing the decision in *Kemper v. Gordon*, 272 S.W.3d 146 (Ky. 2008) to reject the loss of chance doctrine, and showing that the Court's justifications were disputable and debatable); 836 N.W.2d at 349 n. 14; Steven R. Koch, *Whose Loss Is It Anyway? Effects of the "Lost-Chance" Doctrine on Civil Litigation and Medical Malpractice Insurance*, 88 N.C. L. Rev. 595, at 619-27 and 626-30 (2010); and *Fennell v. S. Maryland Hosp. Ctr., Inc.*, 320 Md. 776, 797, 580 A.2d 206, 216 (1990) (Adkins, J., dissenting) ("The elitist notion that Maryland juries would be unable to cope with loss of chance evidence…surely would surprise those who adopted the second paragraph of Article 23 of our Declaration of Rights.").

ccciii. 836 N.W.2d 321; *Alberts v. Schultz*, 126 N.M. 807 (1999); *Delaney v. Cade*, 255 Kan. 199, 218 (1994); *Hamil v. Bashline*, 481 Pa. 256 (1978); *Est. of Frey v. Mastroianni*, 146 Haw. 540 (2020); *Wollen v. DePaul Health Ctr.*, 828 S.W.2d 681 (Mo. 1992); *DeBurkarte v. Louvar*, 393 N.W.2d 131 (Iowa 1986); *Ferrell v. Rosenbaum*, 691 A.2d 641 (D.C. 1997); *Cahoon v. Cummings*, 734 N.E.2d 535 (Ind. 2000); *McMackin v. Johnson Cnty. Healthcare Ctr.*, 2003 WY 91 (Wyo. 2003), *on reh'g* 2004 WY 44 (Wyo. 2004); *Perez v. Las Vegas Med. Ctr.*, 107 Nev. 1 (1991); *Smith v. Providence Health & Servs.-Oregon*, 361 Or. 456 (2017); *McKellips v. Saint Francis Hosp., Inc.*, 1987 OK 69 (1987); *Thompson v. Sun City Cmty. Hosp., Inc.*, 141 Ariz. 597 (1984); *Hastings v. Baton Rouge Gen. Hosp.*, 498 So. 2d 713 (La. 1986); Fangrow, *supra* note 3; Guest, *supra* note 3; and Charles Jones et al., *"The Loss of Chance" Doctrine in Medical Malpractice Cases*, Troutman Pepper (Mar. 13, 2013), www.troutman.com/insights/the-loss-of-chance-doctrine-in-medical-malpractice-cases.html.

ccciv. *Rodriguez v. British Columbia (AG)*, [1993] 3 SCR 519; and *Carter v. Canada (AG)*, 2015 SCC 5, 1 SCR 331.

cccv. 2015 SCC 5.

cccvi. *Id.*

cccvii. *The Canadian Legal System*, The Canada Guide, https://thecanadaguide.com/basics/legal-system/.

cccviii. *See e.g.*, 452 Mass. 1; 272 S.W.3d 146; [1991] 1 SCR 541; [2005] UKHL 2; and 2003 CanLII 50091.

cccix. John Logan, *Spectre*, Scripts, http://www.scripts.com/script-pdf/18640 (last visited Aug. 26, 2022).

cccx.   Habiba Nosheen & Andrew Culbert, *As fewer patients sue their doctor, the rate of winning malpractice suits is dropping too*, CBC (Apr. 18, 2019), www.cbc.ca/news/health/medical-malpractice-doctors-lawsuits-canada-1.4913960 (*note*: these statistics span from 2013-2017 and it is assumed that they have not changed significantly since then); *See also* Douglas Danner, *1 Med. Malprac. Chklsts. & Disc. § 1:11*, Westlaw (database updated Sept. 2021) ("Statistics show that 95% of all medical malpractice cases are dropped, settled or otherwise disposed of before trial. Of the 5% which go to trial, the defendants win about half of these cases."); and Adam C. Schaffer, et al., *Rates and Characteristics of Paid Malpractice Claims Among US Physicians by Specialty*, 1992-2014, JAMA Intern Med. 717 (2017).

cccxi.   Lax Kw'alaams Indian Band v. Canada (AG), 2011 SCC 56, 3 SCR 535.

Thanks for the pirate bed mom....

....and the bread pudding.

Ingram Content Group UK Ltd.
Milton Keynes UK
UKHW051821090723
424713UK00009B/80